# come & die

## THE ANCIENT PATH TO LIFE, HOPE, & FLOURISHING

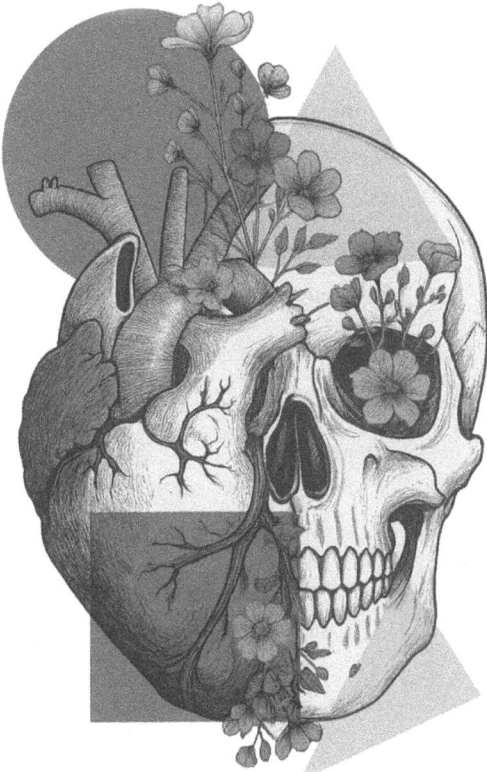

# JAKE TAYLOR

## FOREWORD BY DAVE PATTERSON

"*Come and Die is a bold, timely, and convicting call back to the heart of discipleship. Jake Taylor doesn't sugarcoat the Christian life—he reminds us that it begins with death: death to self, to sin, and to the cultural versions of Jesus that exist only to make us feel better. Through a systematic and Scripture-rich journey into biblical discipleship, Jake shows that true life, hope, and flourishing are found in the way of Jesus. This book is grounded in truth, Scripture, and love—and it speaks directly to the cultural moment we're living in. Jake masterfully balances strong theology with personal story and practical application. His voice is honest, compelling, and deeply pastoral. I highly recommend it to anyone serious about becoming more like Christ.*"

**Jared Ellis- Lead Pastor, E2 Church**

# come & die

## THE ANCIENT PATH TO LIFE, HOPE, & FLOURISHING

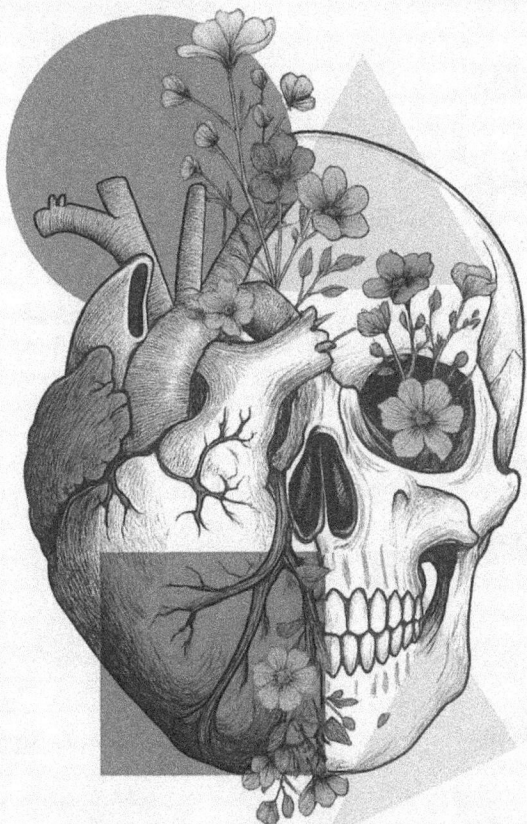

# JAKE TAYLOR

## FOREWORD BY DAVE PATTERSON

# contents

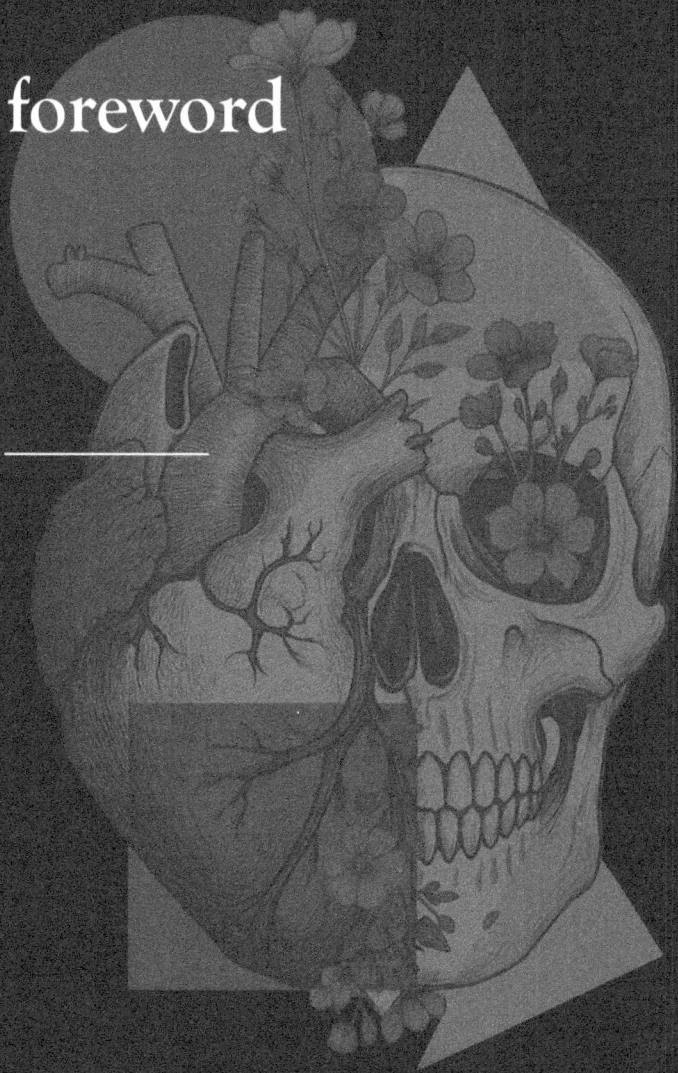

# foreword

———

P astoring a church and leading people out of darkness into the light of Jesus has never been for the faint of heart. The reality of spiritual warfare often overwhelms many pastors, as evidenced by the resignation rate, which is now more than twice that of those being trained and entering full-time ministry. The apostle Paul said it this way, as he described his resume of suffering:

> *Besides those external things, there is the daily, inescapable pressure of my concern for all the churches. (2 Corinthians 11:28,* Amplified)

In this book, Jake Taylor addresses one of Paul's key concerns: the danger of individuals encountering a counterfeit version of the Christian life—one that leaves them disillusioned, unfulfilled, and often drifting back into the very sin and shame they once hoped to escape. The schemes of the enemy have never really changed. His tactic is to mix a debilitating lie with enough truth that the masses easily and readily consume it. The deception and erroneous modern belief system of "self-help-Christianity" has become the "opiate for the masses," especially in our culture of convenience and the quest for self-actualization. This pseudo gospel has promised a result that is unreachable because it does not include the clear requirements of Scripture to be a true follower of Jesus. In this book, Jake does an amazing and thorough job of peeling back the lies and false assumptions regarding the road of a true disciple that have become common to the average church attendee in the 21st century. His heart and goal, in every chapter, is not to beat people down or make them feel like they are not measuring up, but to reintroduce the beauty and simplicity of a life laid down for Jesus, only to be resurrected with purpose, passion, and deep fulfillment.

We have all experienced the frustration of purchasing a product or investing in a treatment that didn't work as expected. You buy into the lie and sign up for the emotional and financial investment, only to realize, months and many dollars later, that you were duped into believing in and purchasing a placebo product. The end result of this cycle is to become cynical and mistrusting of any future product that promises health and healing. Apply this spiritually, and you find the same cycle in people who have been promised spiritual results, yet the main ingredients that bring us from death to life are missing. In the following pages, Jake will lead you, chapter by chapter, to the non-negotiable realities of what Jesus has prescribed for the sin-sick soul, then gracefully unpack the eternal ingredients that will produce the joy, peace, passion, and long-range vision that you were born to experience. I'm excited for you to take this journey!

**Dave Patterson**, Founding Pastor- *The Father's House*

> *"The deception and erroneous modern belief system of "self-help-Christianity" has become the "opiate for the masses," especially in our culture of convenience and the quest for self-actualization."*

# introduction

_____

"*When Christ calls a man,*
*He bids him come and die.*"

**Dietrich Bonhoeffer**

I loved high school. I loved football, rallies, and interacting with teachers who knew they were gifted a platform to mold malleable young minds. I decided that I wanted to be a high school history teacher in my freshman year. I wanted to make an impact on the world, one student at a time, one mind at a time. History has a way of teaching about the future by examining the past. As the old adage goes, *"those who don't know history are doomed to repeat it."*

In my sophomore year of high school, we delved into world history. Ancient History was a snooze; I couldn't care less about ancient Mesopotamia or even the Middle Ages. However, my imagination was awakened as we approached the dawn of the Enlightenment, spanning through the twentieth century. The beginning of a more "civilized time". As we trekked along through the dawn of "progress", the irony was stark; the most "progressive" century was the bloodiest. The rise and fall of dictators and the advent of World War captivated my attention.

World War II was specifically fascinating. I found myself at home reading books, watching movies, and documentaries about it. To this day, if my wife has a night out, chances are I am watching something related to World War II. World War II is a clash of cultures, a collision of worldviews, a fight between good and evil. On one side, you have the heroes' journey played out in reality: the Allied forces storming the beaches of Normandy to an almost certain death, heeding the clarion call of liberty. On the other side: a genocidal maniac who managed to unite a country in despair by providing a proverbial boogeyman to blame for the state of the union. Fascinating.

Before graduating from high school, I came face-to-face with Jesus and realized what my Savior was calling me to. I traded my aim of becoming a high school history teacher for a deeper calling—to shape those same impressionable minds with the life-changing message of the Gospel.

As I dove into theology and learned what it meant to follow Jesus, I stumbled upon a theologian named Dietrich Bonhoeffer. In his biography about Bonhoeffer, Eric Metaxas summarizes his life well, "*Pastor. Martyr. Prophet. Spy.*"[1] Bonhoeffer was not only a theologian but also a pastor in Germany during World War II. He pushed back against the Nazification of the German Church and even played a role in an assassination attempt against Hitler. For that, he was hanged in a concentration camp at the age of 39, two weeks before the Allies liberated that camp. This was history meeting theology.

Perfect.

I started reading Bonhoeffer because of his historical context and continued reading for his theological insights. Bonhoeffer was deeply concerned with the life of the Christian being watered down by "cheap grace." He contrasted *cheap grace* with *costly grace*,

> *Cheap grace is the preaching of forgiveness without repentance, baptism without church discipline, Communion without confession, absolution without personal confession. Cheap grace is grace without discipleship, grace without the cross, grace without Jesus Christ, living and incarnate. Costly*

---

1    Eric Metaxas, *Bonhoeffer* (Nashville, TN: Thomas Nelson, 2010).

*grace is the treasure hidden in the field; for the sake of it a man will gladly go and sell all he has...Costly grace is the gospel which must be sought again and again, the gift which must be asked for, the door at which a man must knock. Such grace is costly because it calls us to follow, and it is grace because it calls us to follow Jesus Christ.*[2]

Bonhoeffer saw the pressures of unredeemed culture pressing in on the church and grimaced as the church acquiesced to a diluted version of discipleship. He stood as a herald, calling the church back to single-hearted devotion to Jesus. Jesus defines what it means to follow Him, no one else. Not me, not society, not the pervading culture.

In this context, Bonhoeffer wrote one of the most influential modern-day definitions of discipleship,

> *"When Christ calls a man, he bids him come and die."*[3]

Bonhoeffer's call to discipleship was an invitation to embrace a 2,000-year-old way of life—an ancient path that leads to life, hope, and flourishing. Though clearly marked, this path is narrow, and few are willing to walk it. Stepping onto it is simple in principle, yet profoundly difficult in practice. To journey down this road—to face its dangers, endure its trials, and press toward its end—is to discover what it means to truly live.

2    Dietrich Bonhoeffer, *The Cost of Discipleship*, (New York; Touchstone, 1937), 45.

3    Bonhoeffer, *The Cost of Discipleship*, 89.

Over the past few centuries, Enlightenment thinking has infiltrated the Church. Abraham Maslow famously developed his *Hierarchy of Needs.* His goal was to dissect human motivation, starting from our basic needs and escalating to the most transcendent. The five levels are *Physiological* (air, water, food, etc.), *Safety* (employment, resources, health, etc.), *Love* (friendship, intimacy, family, etc.), *Esteem* (respect, self-esteem, status, etc.), and *Self-Actualization* (the desire to be *something*). When fused with Christian theology, this philosophical framework turns Jesus into a tool for self-actualization. Jesus exists to make me all I can be. Sociologist Christian Smith refers to this phenomenon as *"moralistic, therapeutic deism."*[4] Discipleship is more of a take than a give. I would argue the lives of many Christians, though they wouldn't say this, demonstrate that Jesus is merely a *"life-enhancer."*

He is the ketchup to their fries.

The A-1 to their poorly cooked steak.

The ice to their lukewarm sweet tea.

Jesus is an accessory.

Jesus is added to their already pre-selected, pre-planned life.

---

4    Christian Smith, Melinda Denton, *Soul Searching: The Religious and spiritual Lives of American Teenagers* (New York: Oxford University Press, 2006).

The more I study Scripture, the more I feel the Spirit of God calling us back, drawing His church back to an accurate understanding of what it means to follow Jesus. To clearly define discipleship using Jesus' definition of what discipleship is. In this book, we will explore three parts, each presenting a big idea about what discipleship is and how it is applied in practice. My goal is to start with first principles. The parts we will discuss are in order of importance: life, hope, and flourishing.

In many ways, I owe this book to Bonhoeffer. He inspired me to dive deeper into Scripture, allowing my Savior to define the process of saving. He lived in a culture that was becoming increasingly syncretistic; the church's theology and the culture's ideology wed as strange bedfellows. Bonhoeffer had the audacity to declare, "*Enough!*"

This book is my way of saying, "*Enough!*" The call to follow Jesus is about Him and not us. Following Jesus means laying down the self, not adding Jesus to our already "perfectly" manicured version of self.

As we begin this journey, I believe Jesus' invitation to the church in Laodicea applies to the modern Western Church. I pray we respond to His invitation.

> Behold, I stand at the door and knock. If anyone hears my voice and opens the door, I will come in to him and eat with him, and he with me.

(Revelation 3:20, ESV)

# Part 1:
# life

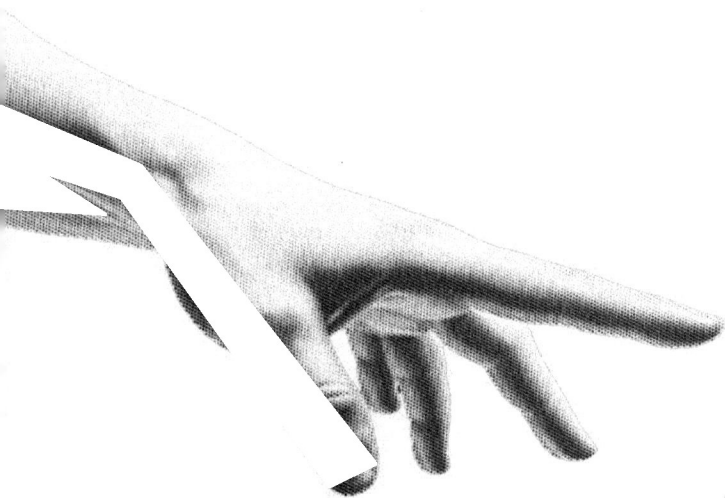

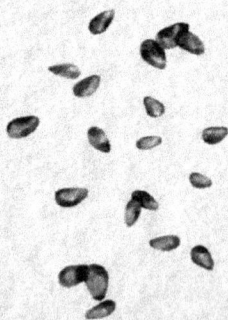

# chapter 1:
# dead as a doorknob

———————

" *Nothing could be more ruthless than to make men think there is still plenty of time to mend their ways.* "

— *Dietrich Bonhoeffer*

My parents are from Arkansas. I was born shortly after they arrived in Sacramento, leaving behind the deep South, with its sweet tea, humidity, and bellowing cicadas. My parents boasted the thickest Southern draw imaginable. My mom's Southern belle persona hid a fiery personality. My dad is the life of the party, hailing from the hills of Arkansas. Think a Jesus-loving, rockstar, and bingo! My earliest memories are of him drumming with the most glorious, permed mullet in the history of humanity. Together, they were and are a power couple.

My dad has always had southernisms: sayings that mean something profound but make no sense to us native born Californians. I heard things like, *"He's got less hope than a one-legged man in a butt kicking contest."* The origin of that reference is a mystery, but it's epic.

Another phrase he often uses is *"dead as a doorknob."* I Googled *"dead as…"* and the first result was *"What does dead as a doorknob mean?"* So, I take it I am not alone. A commenter on a forum explained, *"[a] doorknob* is not alive and never has been–*you can't get any more dead."*

Ah, insight.

Death is a strange thing; we try to avoid it, yet it comes for us all. Biblically and spiritually speaking, all of us either are or have been *"dead as a doorknob."*

## Dead in Sin

The book Ephesians is Paul's letter to the church in Ephesus. Ephesus was a bustling center of commerce, and with a population of 250,000 in the second century, it is believed to have been the third-largest city in the Roman Empire. One of the seven wonders of the ancient world, the Temple of Diana (also known as Artemis), was constructed there. One of the earliest Greek geographers, Strabo, described Ephesus as the largest center for trade west of the Taurus Mountains.[5]

Paul spent three years building the church in Ephesus, and the book of Acts indicates that the work of the ministry was difficult. Embracing Jesus meant turning away from the worship of Artemis, sparking conflict between Christians and idol-makers whose trade suffered because of the emerging Jesus movement. In Acts 19, a mob forms, chanting the odd phrase, *"Great is Artemis of the Ephesians"*. Paul and his companions barely manage to escape alive.

A few years later, he wrote his epistle to the church. Chapter 2 begins with rich theology concerning the human condition pre-Christ,

> *And you were dead in the trespasses and sins in which you once walked, following the course of this world, following the prince of the power of the air, the spirit that is now at work in the sons of disobedience—* (Ephesians 2:1-2, ESV)

Paul, writing to a church that is surrounded by all kinds of pagan revelry, makes it clear that humanity is *dead* in sin.

---

5    Strabo, Geography, trans. Horace Leonard Jones, Loeb Classical Library (Cambridge, MA: Harvard University Press, 1929), 14.1.24.

Not less than optimal.

Not improving.

Not struggling.

Dead.

Dead as a doorknob.

## It's Worse Than You Think

We tend to minimize the scope of the problem. Within the Western Church, we often subconsciously treat Christianity like a spiritual intervention; it's *really just* a behavior modification system. It's where bad people get better and good people get gooder.

Barna research found that 74% of adults agree with the statement, "*…when people are born, they are neither good nor evil – they make a choice between the two as they mature.*"[6]

Nowhere in Scripture do we find this idea. As humans, we aren't basically good people who need a little bit of Jesus seasoning to improve our lack of self-esteem. The overwhelming teaching in the Bible is that we are dead in sin.

We don't need our behavior modified; we need a resurrection.

Sin has killed us.

The concept of sin is absent in many American churches. At the mention of "sin," hair stands on end, keyboard warriors get

---

6    Barna Group, "Americans Draw Theological Beliefs From Diverse Points of View," *Barna*, October 8, 2002, https://www.barna.com/research/americans-draw-theological-beliefs-from-diverse-points-of-view/.

ready to pounce, and progressive ideologs prep their demand for "tolerance." At the same time, many pastors and church leaders hesitate to use "sin" and gravitate toward "mistake", "challenge", or "mishap." The very concept of sin is a roadblock, a mark of demarcation; the belief in such a thing as "sin" separates the culture of the world from the morals of the church.

At least it should.

Sin is the *entire* problem, and repentance is God's antidote.

Before we get there, let's start in Genesis.

## Genesis

In the beginning, God created. He breathes the stars and orders the chaos of the seemingly existent but tumultuous world. God's words and breath spawn life. God desired to create image-bearers to extend the franchise; they would reflect His glory and take dominion over the created order.

> *Then God said, "Let us make man in our image, after our likeness. And let them have dominion over the fish of the sea and over the birds of the heavens and over the livestock and over all the earth and over every creeping thing that creeps on the earth." So God created man in his own image, in the image of God he created him; male and female he created them. And God blessed them. And God said to them, "Be fruitful and multiply and fill the earth and subdue it and have dominion over the fish of the sea and over the birds of the heavens and over every living thing that moves on the earth."* (Genesis 1:26-28, ESV)

> "We don't need our behavior modified; we need a resurrection."

From the beginning, God desired man to reflect Him through bearing His image, and He gave them a job.

Subdue, take dominion!

Also, notice that from the beginning, God converses with man. With the rest of creation, God orders its creation, and it continues on its merry way. With man, God molds; He breathes life into his nostrils. Then, He speaks to him, giving direction, purpose, and clarity to the reason behind his existence. From the beginning, man was designed to hear God and heed His voice.

Of all that God said, one instruction stands apart from the rest,

> And the Lord God commanded the man, "You are free to eat from any tree in the garden; but you must not eat from the tree of the knowledge of good and evil, for when you eat from it you will certainly die." (Genesis 2:16-17, NIV)

Choice is baked into the very essence of God's command. Choose life or choose death. Life follows obedience, death follows disobedience. I imagine most of you know how the story goes: Eve is deceived, Adam is with her, and he signs off on the whole fiasco. Their eyes are opened to their nakedness; shame, and guilt are the results. They attempt to cover themselves with fig leaves, and God finds His image bearers hiding like toddlers who snuck some forbidden cookies.

From that moment forward, sin is infused into the human race. Physical death did not result immediately, but spiritual death did.

Now, there is a chasm between us and our holy God. Acting as our federal head and priest, Adam's sin is transmitted to the rest of humanity. Paul writes in Romans,

> *Therefore, just as sin entered the world through one man, and death through sin, and in this way death came to all people, because all sinned—* (Romans 5:12, NIV)

In layman's terms, this means that not only do we choose to sin, but it is our nature to sin. We are born broken, with a propensity towards rebellion from God.

We do not simply sin by action; we are sinners by nature.

Which means that we are *dead* by nature and in need of *life.*

## Don't Follow Your Heart

In the modern era, a phrase that is rooted in postmodern philosophy and its predecessor, secular materialism, is employed by well-meaning people. That phrase is, *"Follow your heart"* or maybe *"trust your gut."* Though that advice sounds wise, it is a lie dipped in chocolate. At the core of all *"follow your heart"* counsel is a self-centered epistemological standpoint, which means that *the authority for all decisions lies within the self.*

Carl Trueman defines *the self* in his book, *Strange New World,*

> *...the term the self...[is]the deeper notion of where the "real me" is to be found, how that shapes my views of life, and in what the fulfillment or happiness of that "real me" consists.*[7]

---

7    Carl R. Trueman, *"Strange New World",* (Wheaton, IL: Crossway, 2022), 21-22.

He continues to define the zeitgeist of the 21st-century West by stating that the modern self *"assumes the authority of inner feelings and sees authenticity as defined by the ability to give social expression to the same."*[8]

The psychological nature of the modern self is a relatively recent development.

Historically, the self was found in what one was a part of, not what lay between one's ears. Trueman explains in *The Rise and Triumph of the Modern Self* that the self as understood in the modern world is a product of historical processes that have transformed how we think about who we are, shifting from an external, relational identity rooted in God and community to an internal, psychological construct defined by individual experience and desire.[9]

In other words, all other authorities outside of me have become suspect.

I know what's best.

This kind of thinking cannot co-exist with a biblical worldview.

God spoke through the prophet Jeremiah, saying, *"The human heart is the most deceitful of all things, and desperately wicked. Who really knows how bad it is?"* (Jer.17:9, NLT) The heart you're encouraged to trust is *"desperately wicked"*, and it seems we can't even grasp the full extent of its flaws.

---

8    Trueman, *"Strange New World"*, 22.

9    Carl R. Trueman, *"The Rise and Triumph of the Modern Self"*, (Wheaton, IL: Crossway, 2020), 22-23.

Scripture is full of this language. In fact, God wiped out the planet through the Flood stating, *"every inclination of the thoughts of the human heart was only evil all the time"* (Gen. 6:5, NIV) Solomon writes that, *"The hearts of people, moreover, are full of evil and there is madness in their hearts while they live."* (Ecc.9:3, NIV) Then Jesus gives the source of sin, saying,

> *For it is from within, out of a person's heart, that evil thoughts come—sexual immorality, theft, murder, adultery, greed, malice, deceit, lewdness, envy, slander, arrogance, and folly. All these evils come from inside and defile a person.* (Mark 7:21-23, NIV)

In the first three chapters of Romans, Paul sets out to prove the depth of the problem of sin. Chapter one is about how the Gentiles are guilty. Chapter two is about how the Jews, who had the Law, are just as guilty. Chapter three describes how every human on the planet is guilty. Two passages in these first three chapters are particularly pertinent to our discussion. First, Paul summarizes Old Testament teaching on the guilt of humanity by pulling from Old Testament sources,

> *As the Scriptures say,*
> *"No one is righteous—*
> not even one.
> *No one is truly wise;*
> no one is seeking God.
> *All have turned away;*
> all have become useless.
> *No one does good,*
> not a single one."

> *"Their talk is foul, like the stench from an open grave.*
> Their tongues are filled with lies."
> *"Snake venom drips from their lips."*
> *"Their mouths are full of cursing and bitterness."*
> *"They rush to commit murder.*
> *Destruction and misery always follow them.*
> *They don't know where to find peace."*
> *"They have no fear of God at all. (Rom. 3:10-18), NLT*

Then, famously, *"all have sinned and fall short of the glory of God."* (Rom. 3:23, NIV)

So, biblical teaching is clear; sin has infected every facet of humanity. And sinfulness equals spiritual death.

## Raising Toddlers

My wife and I are trying to keep a six-year-old boy and a four-year-old little girl alive. I like to tell people that my son, Levi, is the life of the party; he is all boy and is always on the prowl looking for his next wrestling partner. My little girl Livvy is, let's call it, spicy. I'm planning for her to be a CEO and my retirement plan. I grew up in church and heard about the *idea* of a sin nature my whole life, but it wasn't until I became a parent that I saw that nature play out…from birth. Anyone who has been around little kids knows you don't train sin into them; they come pre-packaged that way. They are born knowing how to fight and bite and steal and scream and put their interests above everyone else's. These kids are Sour Patch Kids, sweet and gentle one minute, punching each other in the face the next.

And they are pastor's kids.

If we are honest, regardless of where you are on your faith journey, an objective look at the world and all that transpires screams, "*Something has gone horribly wrong!*"

What is wrong is *sin.*

Racism=sin.

War= sin.

Poverty= sin.

Abuse= sin.

Sin has infected and affected everything we encounter on this side of eternity. We must come to grips with the enormity of the problem as we begin to discuss what it truly means to follow Jesus.

I am a sinner, and I am dead.

I don't just need a religious behavioral modification program; I require a spiritual resuscitation, and that, above all, is the essence of salvation and the focus of discipleship.

chapter 2:
# exchange

———————

*"Suffering and rejection sum up the whole cross of Jesus. To die on the cross means to die despised and rejected of men."*

**— Dietrich Bonhoeffer**

There's nothing I enjoy more than free stuff. It doesn't matter how useless the free item is; if it's free, I love it. It becomes "*my precious*." My son, Levi, has inherited this trait. He has a basket of assorted goods that he calls his "collection." It's rocks and socks and rally towels from God's favorite NBA team, the Sacramento Kings. It's seashells, it's arcade winnings, it's pennies. It's borderline hoarding. So, my wife and I are working on gently purging his collection to make room for things of actual value.

We are attempting to help him understand what value and cost truly mean. We realized he was starting to grasp the concept when he was taken aback by the prices in Costco.

"*Dad, this is SO expensive!*"

Yes, son—keeping you and your sister alive doesn't come cheap.

When we consider sin and the death that results from it, I think in many ways, we are like my son. We often fail to realize the cost of sin. Or more so, we don't realize the cost required to *pay for* sin.

## Sacrifice

The cost of sin was tangible in the ancient Near East, particularly surrounding the Jewish nation. The Old Testament world centered on paying for sin, and this idea starts in Genesis 3.

When Adam and Eve sinned, they covered themselves with fig leaves. Then, the Bible records that God, seeing their inadequate coverings, replaced them with a better covering: animal skin. So, from the beginning, something had to die, blood had to be shed, to cover the consequences of sin. An innocent animal died to cover Adam and Eve's awareness of their nakedness, which resulted from their sin. Hebrews speaks to this reality, *"without the shedding of blood there is no forgiveness of sins."* (Heb. 9:22, ESV)

After the Exodus, God institutes the tabernacle system as a medium to connect humanity to the divine. Within that system were offerings and sacrifices for various circumstances. The main ones were,

- **The Burnt Offering**: Atonement of sin and dedication to God. The entire animal was consumed, symbolizing God's consumption of the worshipper's whole life.

- **The Grain Offering**: A voluntary offering of gratitude to God

- **Peace Offering**: Expression of friendship and peace with God

- **Sin Offering**: Atonement for unintentional sin

- **Guilt Offering**: Atonement for specific sins committed against God or others

The Jewish people's holiest day of the year was and still is *Yom Kippur*, the *Day of Atonement*. To atone means *"to cover."* The purpose of atonement is *"a covering of sin; the purpose is to accomplish reconciliation between man and God.*[10]   In antiquity, two goats were required; one was sacrificed as the Sin Offering, and the other was known as the Scapegoat; the priest cast lots to determine which goat was which. The Sin Offering was offered on the altar; its blood sprinkled on the mercy seat of the Ark of the Covenant. The priest would then lay his hands on the head of the Scapegoat and confess the sins of Israel. The live goat would be released into the wilderness, *"Symbolically it carried away the sins of the people."*[11]

The idea of cost was built into the tabernacle system. Sin's cost sounded like the bleating of goats and the lowing of cattle. It looked like the altar's fire and blood on the priests' robes. Sin had a visible, audible, tangible cost for those living in the tabernacle/temple system. Sin meant the death of something.

## Logical Sin Map

In Bible college, I had a professor who took the class through a mental exercise to explain the problem of sin. He began by explaining the core purpose of man, which, in its essential design, is a relationship with his Creator. Man was designed to know and be known by God and to love and be loved by God.

Now, this is where I may lose some of my Reformed friends. To live according to design, in relationship with God, requires choice. Love isn't love if it's forced. Love risks choice. As my

---

10    Charles L. Feinberg, "Atonement, Day Of," *Baker Encyclopedia of the Bible* (Grand Rapids, MI: Baker Book House, 1988), 233.

11    Feinberg, "Atonement, Day Of," *Baker Encyclopedia of the Bible*, 233.

professor would say, "*Choice was the risk God was willing to take for love.*"[12]

Relationship requires choice, and choice risks evil. Love and evil are at opposite ends of the choice continuum. Humanity had a will, and God had a will; God desired for those two wills to align. For two willed beings to live in harmony requires an agreed-upon order, which practically looks like law. Yet, a law isn't a law if it isn't enforced or obeyed.

When humanity chose to reject God's law, it violated the order, thus destroying the harmony of wills, and ultimately transgressing against the love relationship, resulting in a separation between God and man. The prophet Isaiah lays this out clearly: "*But your iniquities have made a separation between you and your God, and your sins have hidden his face from you so that he does not hear.*" (Is. 59:2, ESV)

So, sin separates humanity from God.

Keep your philosophical hat on for a moment as we examine the ramifications of this.

The Bible lays out that all life is ultimately an invention of God.

> *See now that I, even I, am he, and there is no god beside me; I kill and I make alive; I wound and I heal; and there is none that can deliver out of my hand.* (Deuteronomy 32:39, ESV)

> *For with you is the fountain of life; in your light do we see light.* (Psalm 36:9, ESV)

> *All things were made through him, and without him was not*
> *anything made that was made. In him was life, and the life*
> *was the light of men.* (John 1:3-4, ESV)

To be separated from God is to be separated from the source
of life. Anything separated from God abides in death. Thus,
sin equals death.

What do we do with that?

How can this conundrum be fixed?

Going back to the temple system, God invented a substitution
system through animal sacrifice. Our spiritual death could
be transferred to a sacrifice, resulting in their physical death.
The theological term is *"imputed"*, which means to *"credit, or*
*attribute[d] to someone."* It was an accounting term used to
transfer debt from one entity to another. The sin of the people
was imputed onto an innocent sacrifice, and the innocence of
the sacrifice was imputed onto the people.

When sin shows up in Genesis, God sacrifices an animal to
create a covering for the nakedness exposed by sin. Meaning,
from the beginning, an exchange of death for life took place.
The Tabernacle and Temple systematized this process, allowing
for the possibility of forgiveness and life to spring from death.

## New Testament Sacrifice

When Jesus steps onto the scene, the sacrificial system is very
much in play. Diaspora Jews from around the known world
would pilgrimage to the temple in Jerusalem for Yom Kippur
to have their sins removed.

# "

"*To be separated from God is to be separated from the source of life.*"

# "

They traveled for divine exchange.

Death for life.

Jesus saw Himself as the ultimate fulfillment of the Sin Offering. Just as the goat of the sin offering was required to be spotless and without blemish, Peter records,

> *...knowing that you were ransomed from the futile ways inherited from your forefathers, not with perishable things such as silver or gold, but with the precious blood of Christ, like that of a lamb without blemish or spot.* (1 Peter 1:18-19, ESV)

John the Baptist, upon seeing Jesus, declared, "*Behold, the Lamb of God, who takes away the sin of the world!*" (John 1:29, ESV)

The prophet Isaiah prophesied with specificity all that the Messiah would endure,

> *But he was pierced for our transgressions;*
> *he was crushed for our iniquities;*
> *upon him was the chastisement that brought us peace,*
> *and with his wounds we are healed.*
> *All we like sheep have gone astray;*
> *we have turned—every one—to his own way;*
> *and the Lord has laid on him*
> *the iniquity of us all.* (Isaiah 53:5-6, ESV)

Throughout His ministry, Jesus repeatedly foretold His coming death and resurrection, consistently connecting His sacrifice to the redemption of humanity. He outlined the ramifications of His sacrifice in the institution of the Lord's Supper.

> *Now as they were eating, Jesus took bread, and after blessing it broke it and gave it to the disciples, and said, "Take, eat; this is my body." And he took a cup, and when he had given thanks he gave it to them, saying, "Drink of it, all of you, for this is my blood of the covenant, which is poured out for many for the forgiveness of sins. (Matt. 26:26-28, ESV)*

Right before the cross, Jesus lays out the doctrine of *Penal Substitutionary Atonement*.

*Penal*: there was a debt that required a penalty to be paid.

*Substitutionary:* Jesus took our place.

*Atonement*: His act of taking our place and paying our penalty brought about atonement, that is, a covering of our sins.

Charles Spurgeon describes this principle,

> *God looks upon us as though that perfect obedience ... had been performed by ourselves ... God considers us as though we were Christ—looks upon us as though his life had been our life—and accepts, blesses, and rewards us as though all that he did had been done by us, his believing people.[13]*

Jesus took on flesh to be one of us. Yet, He did what none of us could: He lived sinlessly. When He died on the cross, He had no sin in and of Himself to pay for; He embodied the sin of humanity. Yet, He was still fully God with the power to pay for sin.

---

13    Charles H. Spurgeon, *"Jehovah Tsidkenu: The Lord Our Righteousness,"* sermon no. 395, preached June 2, 1861, at the Metropolitan Tabernacle, Newington; included in *Metropolitan Tabernacle Pulpit*, vol. 7 (London: Passmore & Alabaster, 1861)

His holiness for my sinfulness.

His healing for my sickness.

His body broken so I could be made whole.

His sacrifice for my forgiveness.

It's the divine exchange.

Paul describes this in 2 Corinthians, "*For our sake he made him to be sin who knew no sin, so that in him we might become the righteousness of God.*" (2 Cor. 5:21, ESV)

Our sin separated us from life, and to be restored to life required death. Jesus died for us so we could live unto God. Salvation is an exchange, a substitution, it's grace.

We cannot understand discipleship without understanding the Cross. The Cross stands at the epicenter of Christianity with all its brutality. Without the sacrifice of Jesus, sin cannot be paid for. Without the Cross, there is no hope, no life, and no future available.

At the Cross, death is exchanged for life.

## King's Game

I love a horrible, heartbreaking team: the Sacramento Kings. For most of my life, they have been a dumpster fire of a franchise. I have a friend who is a lifelong Cleveland Browns fan. We often debate which franchise is worse. Spoiler alert: it's the Kings.

Years ago, a friend of mine called and asked if I wanted to go to a Kings game with him. I was pumped; the Kings were playing the LeBron James, Kyrie Irving-led Cavaliers that night. Both of us were in our late 20s, so I assumed we would be able to sniff heaven from our seats, but hey, we were in the room.

The plan was to meet at his dad's house and then head to the game from there. I grew up middle-class. My parents provided everything we needed and worked their fingers to the bone in order to do so. I guess I subconsciously assumed that my experience was everyone's experience. The moment I pulled up to my friend's dad's house, that belief was challenged. This house was an *estate*. Every room had a theme, its own essence, a *vibe*. The walls smelled like money.

After hanging out in his villa for a while, my friend's dad handed me a parking pass and said, "*See you there.*" So, I loaded up in my Toyota Yaris and headed to the arena. Unbeknownst to me, my assigned parking space was in the lot next to the players' parking lot. So, I backed my Yaris between a Bugatti and a Ferrari and walked towards the front door with some swagger. Shortly after, we were in a lounge *under* the arena. I had never been in a rich person lounge, but I soon discovered that all the refreshments were complimentary. So, I proceeded to load my pockets with Red Vines and hot dogs and waters and slapped warm, moist towelettes on my forehead and neck. I may or may not have made three or four trips back to said rich person lounge to refresh my free-stuff stash.

Not long after, we arrived at our seats, three rows behind the visitors' bench. I was making *eye contact* with LeBron James.

One of the most incredible features of this night was that it cost me *nothing*; it was free. I accepted a free gift. However, that doesn't mean that the tickets were free or that the lounge was free. No, they all had a significant cost, just not to me.

When we talk about salvation, the payment for sin, forgiveness, purpose, and God's mercy, it is free. We are saved by grace alone, through faith alone, in Christ alone. But the free gifts we experience cost Jesus everything.

It cost His blood.

His body.

His mental anguish.

His isolation.

He paid, so we didn't have to.

He paid so we could stand in a place of undeserved privilege.

It's the great exchange.

To understand discipleship, we begin by realizing that we are dead in our sins, and the only way out of this predicament is through the sacrifice of another, through the sacrifice of the God-man. We have the possibility of life because He laid His down. When we recognize the sacrifice paid for our sin, a moment of decision awaits.

chapter 3:
# baby, come back

_____

"*Discipleship means adherence to Jesus Christ alone, and immediately.*"

— **Dietrich Bonhoeffer**

Though Christians and secular humanists are divided on many issues, they typically agree on one thing, at least the spirit of one thing: Jesus was a good teacher. Even if Jesus' claims to divinity are denied and His miracles are relegated to the realm of legend, Jesus seems to have been a genuinely lovely person and was kind to everyone.

He touched lepers.

Kissed the kids.

Held little lambs.

Yet, I would argue that those who reject Christian theology often enjoy Jesus' teachings because they haven't read much of it. If you don't like the teaching of biblical Christianity, you aren't going to like the Christ of the Bible.

In arguably the first Gospel written, the Gospel of Mark[14], the first words of Jesus set the tone for the rest of His ministry:

> *"The time is fulfilled, and the kingdom of God is at hand; repent and believe in the gospel."* (Mark 1:15, ESV)

Jesus begins His ministry in Mark by declaring that the fulfillment of all the Old Testament has come: He is the Messiah who brings the Kingdom of God (the rule and reign of God) in His wake, and the proper, reasonable response to Jesus' arrival is to repent and believe.

Jesus gives the antidote for sin: repentance. The reality of sin underscores the vital importance of repentance.

---

14    Great work is done on the Synoptics in Strauss' work, Mark L. Strauss, *Four Portraits, One Jesus, (Grand Rapids, MI: Zondervan, 2007).*

To this day, when I think of the word repent, I think of a kid I heard "preaching" at my junior college. I remember walking through the quad, hearing a nasally voice rambling incessantly. The closer I got, the more I noticed some guy attempting to tell people about Jesus. With every vein in his forehead protruding, he implored, *"Repent of your sin, you are an enemy of God!"* Although that message is thoroughly biblical,[15] the delivery made my skin crawl. I confronted him, asking where his love for people was. He replied, *"If they are elect, they will respond regardless of how I package the message."*

I would argue that the message of repentance has been tainted by messengers like that guy. When properly understood, repentance is one of the most beautiful gifts God gives to humanity.

## Turn and Agree

Few concepts are as prevalent in Scripture as the concept of repentance. While the Old Testament lacks a direct word-for-word equivalent for the full concept of repentance, its essence is most clearly captured in the word most frequently used: *"return."*

The story of the Old Testament is the story of God setting out on a mission to redeem mankind for His glory. Adam and Eve failed, which shattered their relationship with God; God, in response, promised to take the initiative to restore that relationship. He begins this process in earnest by choosing

---

15    Rom. 5:10.

a man, Abram, who starts a family that becomes a nation, which ultimately brings forth the Messiah. Now, in between the choosing of Abram and that Messiah, there are thousands of years. In this process, God establishes what is known as the Mosaic Covenant. This covenant comes on the heels of God delivering the Hebrew people from slavery in Egypt in miraculous fashion.

For details, see *Prince of Egypt.*

The covenant that God and the Israelites entered into was typical of the Ancient Near East, which often involved a dominant and dominated party, including agreements, stipulations, and blessings or curses for fulfilling or failing to uphold these stipulations. David Campbell notes, "*God takes the place of the conquering king and Israel is the people he conquers or asserts his rulership over.*" Some of the blessings associated with obedience include a bountiful harvest and a blessed land.[16] God promises safety and to fight on their behalf.[17] But above all, He says this:

> *I will look on you with favor and make you fruitful and increase your numbers, and I will keep my covenant with you. You will still be eating last year's harvest when you will have to move it out to make room for the new. I will put my dwelling place among you, and I will not abhor you. I will walk among you and be your God, and you will be my people. I am the LORD your God, who brought you out of*

---

16    Lev. 26:3-5.

17    Lev. 26:6-8.

> *Egypt so that you would no longer be slaves to the Egyptians; I*
> *broke the bars of your yoke and enabled you to walk with heads*
> *held high.* (Leviticus 26:9-13, NIV)

God promises to live in their midst; His very presence will distinguish them from every other nation. Yet, shortly after, the people of Israel begin to drift away. They run after the gods of neighboring nations, enticed to live in a way that grieves God and violates the covenant. As a result, they reap the fruit of sin: pain, separation, and eventually death.

Even still, over and over, God pleads with His people to *return*. Come back to covenant, to obedience, to fidelity. The relationship between Israel and God is likened to a marriage, and God's people are the cheating spouse. One verse in Joel summarizes much of the tone of the prophets,

> *Rend your heart and not your garments. Return to*
> *the* LORD *your God, for he is gracious and compassionate,*
> *slow to anger and abounding in love, and he relents from*
> *sending calamity.* (Joel 2:13, NIV)

Throughout the Old Testament, God raises up leaders, judges, kings, and prophets to call His people back to obedience and relationship. Baked into the word *"return"* is the idea of realizing the error of your ways, agreeing with God's way, and choosing to obey God instead.

Another Hebrew word often translated as *"repent"* is *nāḥam,* which means *to regret or feel remorse.*[18]

---

18    James Swanson, *Dictionary of Biblical Languages with Semantic Domains: Hebrew (Old Testament)* (Oak Harbor: Logos Research Systems, Inc., 1997).

It is even translated as *"change your mind"* as in Numbers 23:19:

> *God is not human, that he should lie, not a human being, that he should change his mind…* (Numbers 23:19, NIV)

In this context, the Bible essentially says God *"repented."* Clearly, we are not talking about sin in this example; God is perfect and incapable of sin, thus has no need to repent. But we get a snapshot of the concept of repentance. So far, to repent means: *to change your mind and to change your direction.*

When Jesus calls to the crowds, imploring them to *repent* in Mark 1, He is calling for a change of mind, followed by a change of direction. Repentance forces us to realize that we are not the center of authority; God is. We don't know what is best; God does. We don't know what is right and proper and good in and of ourselves. God is right and proper, and good in and of Himself. Repentance is a surrender of authority, an owning of our sin, a change of direction, a return to Jesus. To follow Jesus is to live a lifestyle of repentance. To understand the concept of repentance for what it truly is —a gift from God —we *must* first acknowledge that we have things to repent for.

## Standpoint Epistemology

We live at an interesting point in history. The philosophical underpinnings behind *how* we think and *what* we think are unique. Our means and manner of arriving at what is true have changed. The philosophical study of how we determine what is true is known as *epistemology.* In the West, our culture is shaped by *standpoint epistemology or standpoint theory,* which has been defined as *"a… theoretical perspective that argues that knowledge stems from social position."* Standpoint theory stems from a combination of Marxist and Third-Wave feminist thought, essentially placing the locus of authority on the self, which we discussed above. Risking over-simplification, standpoint theory posits that each individual is the author of what is true and right and good based on their lived experience and the various intersections of their oppressed identities. It bypasses an absolute truth or an objective reality and believes, *"Knowledge is socially situated – knowledge is based on experience, and different situations result in different knowledges."*[19] Many proponents of Standpoint Theory are not opposed to teasing out what corresponds with reality through further research. Yet skepticism behind the knowability of objective truth lingers.

When a culture relocates the authority to determine truth from objective reason and science to the individual's lived experience, disaster is imminent. What happens when *my truth* and *your truth* collide? What happens when what I espouse to be reality and what you believe to be fact are irreconcilably different? We get the climate of America in 2025.

The concept of *sin* does not compute for those who cling to Standpoint Theory wholesale.

---

19   Sandra Harding. "Introduction: Standpoint Theory as a Site of Political, Philosophic, and Scientific Debate" in *The Feminist Standpoint Theory Reader: Intellectual & Political Controversies*, 2004, New York and London: Routledge, 1-15.

If I decide what is true, then *nothing* is inherently wrong. Morality becomes the powerful dictating to the weak what they dislike.

Thomas Hobbes espoused this mode of thinking when he wrote,

> *Moral philosophy is nothing else but the science of what is good, and evil, in the conversation, and society of mankind. Good, and evil, are names that signify our appetites, and aversions; which in different tempers, customs, and doctrines of men, are different.*[20]

Hobbes suggests that what we call evil and good are simply titles we give to "*appetites and aversions.*" In other words, evil is what we don't like; good is what we like. Objective right and wrong do not exist.

The world we live in today is the culmination of a moral free-for-all and an outright rejection of the moral principles laid out in the Judeo-Christian ethic. So, to bring it back around, the preaching of *sin,* both my innate sin nature and my sinful actions, is offensive to the prevailing culture, which outright rejects objective morality. In layman's terms, culture does not believe in sin, thus repentance need not apply.

And this is where the message of Jesus collides with the spirit of the age. Jesus' invitation was simple:

> *The Kingdom of God is here; your proper response to this arriving Kingdom is to repent of your sin and believe.*

At the risk of repetition, sin is the problem, and repentance is God's antidote.

---

20    Thomas Hobbes. *"The Essential Leviathan: A Modernized Edition",* *(Indianapolis:* Hackett Publishing, 2016), 87.

"*The Kingdom of God is here; your proper response to this arriving Kingdom is to repent of your sin and believe.*"

## Defining Repentance

Bearing all that in mind, what is a comprehensive definition of repentance? To answer this question, I will channel my inner Baptist and give you four C's.

1. *Conviction of the Holy Spirit*

   *"One of the most fundamental marks of true repentance is a disposition to see our sins as God sees them."[21]*

First and foremost, repentance is a *gift* from the Holy Spirit. Repentance begins with the Spirit of God pressing on our spirit, enlightening our understanding, and urging us to change. Conviction is an act of God's grace. Conviction highlights where we are falling short and pleads with us to live up to the standard of God.

Before the Passion week, Jesus promised the Holy Spirit would perform this action in the life of His disciples,

> *But very truly I tell you, it is for your good that I am going away. Unless I go away, the Advocate will not come to you; but if I go, I will send him to you. When he comes, he will prove the world to be in the wrong about sin and righteousness and judgment...* (John 16:7-8, NIV)

From the very birth of the Church, the Holy Spirit began to fulfill this promise. After Peter preaches his first message, Acts records that, *"When the people heard this, they were cut to the heart and said to Peter and the other apostles, 'Brothers, what*

---

21  Charles Simeon. *Sermon on Repentance*. Preached at Holy Trinity Church, Cambridge.

*shall we do?"* (Acts 2:37, NIV) God, in His kindness, pricks our hearts, urges us to turn away from sin, from death, and towards Him.

2.    *Contrition of the Heart*

> *"Man is born with his back toward God. When he truly repents, he turns right around and faces God. Repentance is a change of mind.... Repentance is the tear in the eye of faith."* [22]

God designed us with emotions, intentionally. When the conviction of the Holy Spirit comes, it touches our emotions. True repentance requires our emotional involvement.

In the gospel of Luke, Jesus uses a parable to teach His disciples about prayer and righteousness. In the parable, two men go to the temple to pray. One, a Pharisee, is confident in his righteousness; His prayer centers on boasting about his moral purity and thanking God that he isn't like all the other scumbag people around him. In contrast, the other man is a tax collector. Jesus describes him by saying, *"But the tax collector stood at a distance. He would not even look up to heaven, but beat his breast and said, 'God, have mercy on me, a sinner."* (Luke 18:13, NIV) Can you guess which one Jesus praises? The tax collector had an accurate assessment of his guilt before God. Jesus said he beat his breast; this speaks of grief and contrition in his emotions.

---

22    Dwight L. Moody, George Sweeting, Who Said That? (Chicago: Moody Press, 1995), 375.

Paul writes in 2 Corinthians that there is such a thing as godly sorrow. God actually *wants* us to feel the pain of sin in our emotions. Paul says, "*For godly grief produces a repentance that leads to salvation without regret, whereas worldly grief produces death.*" (2 Corinthians 7:10, ESV) True repentance begins with the nudging of the Holy Spirit, prompting us to change our ways and align with God's truth. That nudge is felt in our emotions.

### 3.  Confession of the Mouth

> "*The beginning of repentance is the confession of guilt.*"[23]

True repentance leads to confession. We own our sin by confessing it. Unconfessed sin is unrepentant sin. We confess in two ways:

### A.  To God

First and foremost, we confess our sins to God. We acknowledge verbally that we have violated His ways, and we ask for forgiveness and the strength to submit to His lordship. The psalmist declares,

> *Then I acknowledged my sin to you*
> *and did not cover up my iniquity.*
> *I said, "I will confess my transgressions to the LORD."*
> *And you forgave the guilt of my sin.* (Psalm 32:5, NIV)

---

23  John Calvin, *Commentaries on the Book of the Prophet Jeremiah and the Lamentations*, vol. 1, trans. John Owen (Edinburgh: Calvin Translation Society, 1850), 153.

This theme is continued in John's first epistle, where he writes, *"If we confess our sins, he is faithful and just to forgive us our sins and to cleanse us from all unrighteousness."* (1 John 1:9, ESV)

### B. To Others

This is the point where genuine repentance often ends. Genuine repentance includes confessing to God and confessing to others. James writes about a unique benefit accessed by confession within the community: *"Therefore confess your sins to each other and pray for each other so that you may be healed. "(James 5:16a, NIV)*

Only God can forgive sin, but God has chosen interpersonal confession as a means to produce *healing*. I have heard it said, *"Many Christians are forgiven, but not many are healed."*

Genuine repentance begins with the conviction of the Holy Spirit, which is felt in our emotions, leading to confession to God, where we ask for forgiveness. Then, genuine repentance brings other people into the equation for healing and accountability.

### 4. Confrontation of the Will

*"True repentance does not consist merely in the feeling and confession of sin, but in the amendment of life and the sincere turning to God."* [24]

---

24   Martin Luther, *The Large Catechism*, in *Luther's Works*, vol. 38, ed. Helmut T. Lehmann (Philadelphia: Fortress Press, 1959), 312.

This is where the rubber meets the road. Repentance isn't repentance if there is no change of action. Our will must be changed to align with God's.

In other words, you choose to obey what God has commanded, deliberately turning away from the desires of your sinful nature and aligning yourself with His will. It means surrendering your own will and actions to God, living in obedience to Him. You embody the heart of the Lord's Prayer: "*Your kingdom come; your will be done on earth as it is in heaven.*"

## Returning Home

I remember getting mad at my parents for something when I was seven. I don't know what it was; they probably turned off Super Mario Brothers on my Super Nintendo or insisted I refrain from punching one of my younger siblings. Although the reason for my anger eludes me, I remember packing a backpack full of clothes and thinking, "*I am out of here, I am doing things my way.*" I snuck out the front door and made it down the street. I had an incredible plan in my head; I was off to see the world. *"Maybe I'll stop in Tokyo first, no, Paris."* Eventually, I'd need to commit myself to embracing the destiny I was crafted for before the foundation of the world: I was to be the second coming of Michael Jordan. Unfortunately, twenty minutes later, I missed home, I missed my parents, and I realized my seven-year-old brain was moronic, so I returned home.

The work of Jesus on the Cross has opened a way home, a way to stop rebelling, to stop settling for death, and to realize you were created, wired for *life*. Repentance is just that: *a return home.*

*Home* is living according to design.

*Home* is living God's way.

Our souls crave our design.

To rage against design, against God's way, is to rage against *home*.

The Spirit of God is that homesick feeling in your soul. That deep sense of knowing that there is more than *this*. You were not created for this world; you just live here. Saint Augustine famously said,

> *...you made us for yourself, and our hearts find no peace until they rest in you.*[25]

Our hearts cannot rest in God until true, genuine repentance is walked out. But when it is, at this point, the Spirit of God does what He is so good at doing: He brings *life*.

---

25    Augustine of Hippo, *Confessions,* trans. Henry Chadwick (Oxford: Oxford University Press, 1991), 3.

# chapter 4:
## "clear!"

_____

_"The call to discipleship, the baptism
in the name of Jesus Christ means both
death and life."_

— **Dietrich Bonhoeffer**

For whatever reason, my wife and I gravitate towards dramatic medical shows. Over the past decade, we have watched too many to count.

Grey's Anatomy.

The Resident.

911.

Frequently, in the heat of the ER, a patient's heart will stop beating, prompting a nurse or resident to boldly assert, "*They're coding!*" Without fail, calls ring for a defibrillator. We all know the scene, "*Charge to 200. Clear!*" BAM! Tears are shed as the nearly dead patient is brought back to life.

Following Jesus is first and foremost a "*CLEAR!*" moment. All humanity is lying on that table. There is no spiritual sinus rhythm. We aren't coding; we *have coded*. In following Jesus, death is turned to life.

In explaining the concept of death to life, I want to break down the work of the Holy Spirit and the work of the Cross. God eternally exists in three persons: Father, Son, and Holy Spirit. All are co-equal, co-God, co-eternal. As an excerpt from the Athanasian Creed states,

> *Now this is the catholic faith:*
>
> *That we worship one God in trinity and the trinity in unity,*
> *neither blending their persons*
> *nor dividing their essence.*
> *For the person of the Father is a distinct person,*
> *the person of the Son is another,*

*and that of the Holy Spirit still another.*
*But the divinity of the Father, Son, and Holy Spirit is one,*
*their glory equal, their majesty coeternal.*

*What quality the Father has, the Son has, and the Holy Spirit has.*
*The Father is uncreated,*
*the Son is uncreated,*
*the Holy Spirit is uncreated.*

*The Father is immeasurable,*
*the Son is immeasurable,*
*the Holy Spirit is immeasurable.*

*The Father is eternal,*
*the Son is eternal,*
*the Holy Spirit is eternal.*

*And yet there are not three eternal beings*

*there is but one eternal being....*

They all worked together in the process of redemption. In tandem, they accomplished the opportunity for mankind's salvation.

The most famous verse in the Bible is in the context of Jesus explaining the process of salvation to a religious leader. Nicodemus was a Pharisee, and as such, he was respected and revered by the people. This influential and revered leader shows up to ask Jesus some questions... at night. He waits until crowds dissipate, the bustle of city streets has quieted, and his adoring fans are nowhere to be seen. Then, and only then, does he approach this apparent iconoclast, Jesus the Nazarene.

In this conversation, Nicodemus begins with platitudes and religious niceties for which Jesus has no time. He slices right through the religious jargon, saying, *"Very truly I tell you, no one can see the kingdom of God unless they are born again."* (John 3:3, NIV) Nicodemus is taken aback. How can one be physically born again?

What is this madman referring to?

Jesus reveals the salvific teamwork between Him and the Spirit; He lays down His life as a ransom for many, while the Spirit gives birth to new, fresh life. Jesus would pay the price for salvation, the Holy Spirit would do the work of leading to truth, convicting of sin, and applying the spiritual defibrillator to dead humanity.

Jesus specifically details, *"Truly, truly, I say to you, unless one is born of water and the Spirit, he cannot enter the kingdom of God. That which is born of the flesh is flesh, and that which is born of the Spirit is spirit."* (John 3:5-6, ESV)

Paul expounds on this concept throughout his letters to the churches,

> *...Anyone who does not have the Spirit of Christ does not belong to him. (Romans 8:9b, ESV)*

> *And hope does not put us to shame, because God's love has been poured into our hearts through the Holy Spirit who has been given to us. (Romans 5:5, ESV)*

> *But we ought always to give thanks to God for you, brothers beloved by the Lord, because God chose you as the firstfruits to be saved, through sanctification by the Spirit and belief in the truth. (2 Thessalonians 2:13, ESV)*

> *And such were some of you. But you were washed, you were sanctified, you were justified in the name of the Lord Jesus Christ and by the Spirit of our God.* (1 Corinthians 6:11, ESV)

> *For if you live according to the flesh you will die, but if by the Spirit you put to death the deeds of the body, you will live. For all who are led by the Spirit of God are sons of God. For you did not receive the spirit of slavery to fall back into fear, but you have received the Spirit of adoption as sons, by whom we cry, "Abba! Father!" The Spirit himself bears witness with our spirit that we are children of God...* (Romans 8:13-16, ESV)...

The role of the Holy Spirit is vital. The Holy Spirit acts as the purifier, the regenerator, the seal, and the adopter. We will discuss this later, but when God saves you, He adopts you.

## Pastoral Epistles

Paul has a category of his letters known as the Pastoral Epistles, which were written to his sons in the Lord, Titus and Timothy. These men pastored local congregations and had local church questions. Throughout these letters, Paul provides practical ministry instructions, guidance on selecting leaders, and, above all, emphasizes the vital importance of correct doctrine. Over and over and over, Paul implores these local church pastors to guard sound Christian teaching. Then, in a few places, he provides some of the sound teaching that must be guarded.

Titus, an uncircumcised Greek Christian serving as a pastor on the island of Crete, was a unique figure. Crete itself was conquered and brought under Roman rule in 67 BC; its strategic position, situated between Greece, Egypt, and the eastern Mediterranean coastal region, established it as a vibrant center for trade and cultural exchange. The island's culture blended a notorious array of pastimes, including piracy and the employment of mercenaries. At the same time, its religion incorporated diverse pagan influences, including the worship of Augustus, Roma, Asclepius, Isis, and Serapis. Paul's letter reflects a young Christian community struggling with false teachers, possibly Jewish converts blending local myths with doctrine, and a culture Paul critiques by quoting a legendary local poet, Epimenides, who said, "*Cretans are always liars, evil beasts, lazy gluttons*" (Titus 1:12)

The epistle to Titus reflects the tender heart of a father, as Paul yearns for Titus to thrive and, upon entering eternity, hear, "*Well done, my good and faithful servant.*"

Among many theological diatribes, Paul inserts this important salvific description,

> *For we ourselves were once foolish, disobedient, led astray, slaves to various passions and pleasures, passing our days in malice and envy, hated by others and hating one another. But when the goodness and loving kindness of God our Savior appeared, he saved us, not because of works done by us in righteousness, but according to his own mercy, by the washing of regeneration and renewal of the Holy Spirit, whom he poured out on us richly through Jesus Christ our Savior, so that being justified by his grace we might become heirs according to the hope of eternal life.* (Titus 3:3-7, ESV)

This description perfectly sums up what we have discussed in this book so far. His readers were:

1.   Sinful

2.   Saved by the work of Jesus

3.   Regenerated and Renewed by the Holy Spirit

This last point is what I want to camp on to conclude this chapter. When the Bible says we have been renewed and regenerated by the Holy Spirit, what does that mean?

1.   Regeneration

Within the context of this passage, Paul begins by outlining the actions of our depraved nature, "[we were] *foolish, disobedient, led astray, slaves to various passions and pleasures, passing our days in malice and envy, hated by others and hating one another…*" He is making one thing clear: left to our own devices, humans do bad stuff.  In this context, he pivots to God's actions:

God showed His goodness.

God showed His kindness.

God did the saving.

The work of regeneration *begins* with God, an act of grace, that is, undeserved favor.  We don't deserve it or earn it; we simply respond to what God has done.

Now, let's define terms. Regeneration refers to the "*experience of a complete change of life.*"[26] Paul speaks of the work of the

26   William Arndt et al., *A Greek-English Lexicon of the New Testament and Other Early Christian Literature* (Chicago: University of Chicago Press, 2000), 752.

Spirit being a "*bath of regeneration and renewal by the Holy Spirit.*"[27] One Bible Dictionary defines regeneration as the exact concept we have been discussing: "*The transformation of a person's spiritual condition from death to life through the work of the Holy Spirit.*"[28]

The concept of regeneration was present in Greek thought through the likes of Plato and Pythagoras. Greek regeneration, however, was different. For example,

> *Plato records Socrates recounting how souls, after being separated from their bodies, spend an indefinite period of time in Formland and then return to Earth, assuming new bodies.*[29]

In the Old Testament, the word "*regeneration*" does not appear, but the concept is present. Famously, God spoke through Ezekiel, saying,

> *And I will give you a new heart, and a new spirit I will put within you. And I will remove the heart of stone from your flesh and give you a heart of flesh. And I will put my Spirit within you and cause you to walk in my statutes and be careful to obey my rules.* (Ezekiel 36:26-27)

Even in Deuteronomy, the concept of regeneration is present, as God declares,

27    Arndt., *A Greek-English Lexicon of the New Testament and Other Early Christian Literature*, 752.

28    Kirk R. MacGregor, "Regeneration," in *The Lexham Bible Dictionary*, ed. John D. Barry et al. (Bellingham, WA: Lexham Press, 2016).

29    MacGregor, "Regeneration," in *The Lexham Bible Dictionary*.

*And the LORD your God will circumcise your heart and the heart of your offspring, so that you will love the LORD your God with all your heart and with all your soul, that you may live.* (Deuteronomy 30:6, ESV)

Fast forward to the New Testament, and these prophecies are fulfilled. Through the atoning sacrifice of Jesus, our sins have been paid for in full, the door is open, and the Holy Spirit moves upon our faith and transforms our *"soul from estrangement from God to right relationship with Him."* [30]

Merrill Frederick Unger defines regeneration as *"a change in our moral and spiritual nature."* [31] He goes on to say, "[regeneration] *is the change from the state of depravity, or spiritual death, to that of spiritual life."* [32]

In other words, regeneration is the Holy Spirit applying the defibrillator.

### 2.    Renewal

Notice, Paul highlights two actions taken by the Holy Spirit: He regenerates, and He renews.

Regeneration is the defibrillator that brings you back to life; renewal is the physical therapy that trains you to walk as you were meant to. Regeneration wakes you up to the reality of God; renewal trains you to walk in the ways of God.

---

30    MacGregor, "Regeneration," in *The Lexham Bible Dictionary*.

31    Merrill Frederick Unger et al., *The New Unger's Bible Dictionary* (Chicago: Moody Press, 1988).

32    Unger, *The New Unger's Bible Dictionary*.

Not only does the Holy Spirit breathe life into us, but He also takes up residence within the believer. Jesus outlines this aspect of the person of the Holy Spirit, saying,

> *And I will ask the Father, and he will give you another Helper, to be with you forever, even the Spirit of truth, whom the world cannot receive, because it neither sees him nor knows him. You know him, for he dwells with you and will be in you.* (John 14:16-17, ESV)

We'll explore this truth in more detail later, but for now, let me note that salvation marks the start of a transformative journey to become more like Jesus through the power of the Holy Spirit.

The Holy Spirit empowers, speaks to, leads, guides, convicts, challenges, corrects, comforts, gifts, and teaches.

## Conclusion

The Bible outlines the process of salvation in a straightforward manner. All humanity is dead in sin with a nature that needs a supernatural spark from the Creator. Just as God spoke to bring order out of chaos and life appeared from the depths of darkness in the beginning, so the Holy Spirit breathes again to bring life from death in the heart of fallen humanity. When the Gospel message is preached, the Spirit of God hovers over the water of the hearts of dead humanity, bringing conviction, a deep-seated "knowing" that the message about who Jesus is and what He has done is true. In that moment, an opportunity arises:

"*In other words, regeneration is the Holy Spirit applying the defibrillator.*"

*"Will I repent, turn from my sin, accept Jesus' payment for that sin, and follow Jesus? Or will I ignore the Spirit of God and continue in depravity?"* When true repentance occurs, the Spirit of God moves, and what was dead is brought to life. The sin nature is replaced with a nature that desires to please God; the process of becoming like Jesus begins.

To begin to follow Jesus is to begin at the beginning. Following Jesus starts with resurrection. Before I can walk with Jesus, I must be brought to life.

Following Jesus means, first and foremost, realizing that Jesus alone can bring me back to life. Salvation is the process by which we see the error of our ways, agree with God, walk in repentance, and accept the gift of new life from the Holy Spirit. And with that life, that sweet, abundant life, comes hope.

> *When you were dead in your sins and in the uncircumcision of your flesh, God made you alive with Christ. He forgave us all our sins, having canceled the charge of our legal indebtedness, which stood against us and condemned us; he has taken it away, nailing it to the cross. And having disarmed the powers and authorities, he made a public spectacle of them, triumphing over them by the cross* (Col.2:13-15, NIV)

part 2:

# hope

# chapter 5:
# having fun yet?

———————

*"To endure the cross is not a tragedy; it is the suffering which is the fruit of an exclusive allegiance to Jesus Christ."*

— **Dietrich Bonhoeffer**

Now that we have examined the '*why we need saving*' element of discipleship —the '*we are dead and need to be brought to life*' part —let's look at what happens next. Once I have surrendered my life to Jesus by acknowledging His divinity and sacrifice, accompanied by the fruit of confession and a turning away from sin, something else happens: hope is born.

The world is a weird place; beauty and anguish exist side by side. I will never forget the first time I drove into Tijuana, Mexico. On one side of the border are multi-million-dollar homes boasting oceanside views and laid-back living. On the other side, families of five or six scrape together whatever materials they can to craft makeshift shacks. The separation between wealth and poverty, excess and starvation is less than a mile wide.

That's like our experience on Earth. Pleasure and anguish, beauty and ashes, depression and joy, often so close they could kiss. Pain is a part of life. As I introduce *hope* into the discipleship equation, I want to take this chapter to talk about suffering. Which I know sounds weird.

"*You start talking about hope by talking about suffering?*"

Just hold your horses and stay with me.

We start following Jesus because we need life, and hope is one of the first byproducts produced by the Holy Spirit. We need hope because *life is hard*. In fact, Jesus promised that it would be.

## Trials are Coming

The Gospel of John is unique among the Gospels. Matthew, Mark, and Luke are known as the Synoptics due to the similarity of their content. Then we get John. John does his own thing; he has his own theological bone to pick. John wants the reader to understand Jesus' deity, which is why he begins with a unique genealogy. Unlike the ones found in Matthew and Luke, John's genealogy is the divine genealogy.

> *In the beginning was the Word, and the Word was with God and the Word was God. He was with God in the beginning. Through him all things were made; without him nothing was made that has been made. In him was life, and that life was the light of all mankind. The light shines in the darkness, and the darkness has not overcome it.* (John 1:1-5, NIV)

Throughout John, the divine nature of Jesus is shown. Fast forward to the end of the book, and interestingly, John chooses to spend chapters 13 through 17 recording Jesus' last Passover meal with His disciples. Jesus washes their feet, predicts His betrayal, prophesies Peter's denial, and clearly articulates His mission and goal: He will leave to prepare a place for them, yet they are to remember that He is *the* way, *the* truth, and *the* life. He then promises the infilling of the third person of the Trinity, the Holy Spirit. The Spirit will lead them, guide them, give them words to say, and reveal truth.

In this portion of Scripture, Jesus repeatedly encourages the disciples not to fear or be troubled.

- *"Do not let your hearts be troubled."* (John 14:1, NIV)

- *"Do not let your hearts be troubled and do not be afraid."* (John 14:27, NIV)

- *"But take heart!* (John 16:33b, NIV)

One specific phrase Jesus uses is key to our discussion,

*"I have told you these things, so that in me you may have peace. In this world you will have trouble. But take heart! I have overcome the world." (John 16:33, NIV)*

The back half of chapter 15 and all of chapter 16 detail the suffering, persecution, pain, and grief associated with being a faithful follower of Jesus. Then, to cap it off, we get a promise from Jesus, *"In this world you will have trouble."* Jesus promises trouble, promises persecution. In fact, for good measure, let me give you a summary of each time He says suffering will happen in these chapters:

- If the world hates you, remember that it hated me first. (John 15:18, NIV)

- I have chosen you out of the world. That is why the world hates you. (John 15:19b, NIV)

- If they persecuted me, they will persecute you. (John 15:20b, NIV)

- The time is coming when anyone who kills you will think they are offering a service to God. (John 16:2, NIV)

- Very truly I tell you, you will weep and mourn while the world rejoices. (John 16:20a, NIV)

- In this world, you will have trouble. (John 16:33b, NIV)

Feeling encouraged yet?

Imagine this scene: Jesus sits at the table with His disciples, fully aware that this meal marks their final gathering, and it is within this intimate moment that He foretells the suffering that lies ahead. Life has come through Jesus the Savior, but that doesn't mean everything in the here and now has been "fixed." On this side of eternity, suffering is a part of the journey.

## Suffering in the Bible

Suffering is all over the Bible. Jacob is mistreated, despite serving Laban faithfully. Joseph is sold into slavery and then thrown in prison for being faithful to God. The Israelites endured 400 years of slavery in Egypt. The Psalter is littered with lamentations about how the righteous suffer while the wicked appear to prosper. This is not even to mention the whole Job saga or the prophets' enduring hardship and suffering for doing *precisely* what God told them to do. In fact, it says this in Hebrews,

> *Some faced jeers and flogging, and even chains and imprisonment. They were put to death by stoning; they were sawed in two; they were killed by the sword. They went about in sheepskins and goatskins, destitute, persecuted and mistreated—the world was not worthy of them. They wandered in deserts and mountains, living in caves and in holes in the ground. These were all commended for their faith.* (Heb. 11:36-39, NIV)

Hebrews 11 is known as *The Hall of Faith*. The characters described in v.36-39 are heroes of the faith who lived lives of faithful obedience to God. Yet, suffering resulted.

What do we do with that?

To stay on this encouraging note, let's look at Paul's life. Paul wrote thirteen of the twenty-seven books in the New Testament. Paul traveled all over the known world, preaching the gospel and planting churches. He moved in power and was used by the Holy Spirit, obeying God's call throughout. Yet, he records his ministry experience this way,

> *I have worked much harder, been in prison more frequently, been flogged more severely, and been exposed to death again and again. Five times I received from the Jews the forty lashes minus one. Three times I was beaten with rods, once I was pelted with stones, three times I was shipwrecked, I spent a night and a day in the open sea, I have been constantly on the move. I have been in danger from rivers, in danger from bandits, in danger from my fellow Jews, in danger from Gentiles; in danger in the city, in danger in the country, in danger at sea; and in danger from false believers. I have labored and toiled and have often gone without sleep; I have known hunger and thirst and have often gone without food; I have been cold and naked. Besides everything else, I face daily the pressure of my concern for all the churches. (2 Cor. 11:23-28, NIV)*

Paul writes to the church in Corinth, recording what it means to be an apostle. It's not pomp and circumstance; it's not about green rooms and popularity or honorariums. The true mark of an apostle is suffering. I would take it a step further: the true mark of a *disciple*, a *follower of Jesus*, is suffering. Our world—all we experience on this side of eternity—is marred in and broken by sin. Though we are saved, we still experience that brokenness as we interact with the world. Thus, understanding the nature of suffering is vital to the follower of Jesus.

I grew up in church and have seen more people than I care to count turn their backs on Jesus. I believe a good portion of them did so because following Jesus didn't look like they wanted it to look. They envisioned Jesus swooping in to save them from all pain, all trials, all hardship. A common complaint I have heard is, "*I turned to Jesus, and life got harder!*"

Which is probably true.

In my mind, the causes of suffering are twofold: sin, both personal and the brokenness of this world, and spiritual warfare. When we sin, there are ramifications. Additionally, there is the prevalent sinfulness of the world and the resulting brokenness that follows from broken systems.

Also, spiritual warfare is real. Just like there is a very real God, the Creator, there is a very real enemy, Satan, who "*prowls around like a roaring lion looking for someone to devour.*" (1 Pet. 5:8, NIV) We will delve into this more in the next chapter, but when the Holy Spirit regenerates you, a transfer of Kingdoms takes place. You are transferred from the Kingdom of Darkness to the Kingdom of Light.[33] That enemy is not a fan of deserters. So, spiritual attacks are real.

33    Col. 1:13

## Suffering is Productive

Now, this is where we get to hope. Though there is suffering and pain on this side of eternity, for those of us who are followers of Jesus, God uses suffering as an agent for growth. Let's break down three things that are produced when we suffer well.

### 1.  Nearness to God

Let's go back to Paul recounting his suffering. After the portion we read, he goes on in chapter twelve to famously talk about his *thorn in the flesh*. We don't know exactly what it was, but Paul specifically calls it a *"messenger of Satan, to torment me."* (1 Cor. 12:7, NIV) Paul asked God to take it away three times, and God's response is, *"My grace is sufficient for you, for my power is made perfect in weakness."* (1 Cor. 12:9, NIV) Jesus lays out for Paul that, although he is suffering and his prayer is not being answered in the manner he would like, there is a level of the grace and power of God that can only be accessed through suffering. When we suffer, we experience new levels of the sufficiency of Jesus. The Psalmist famously said, *"The Lord is close to the brokenhearted."* (Ps. 34:18a, NIV) There is a level of closeness to God that can only be accessed through pain and suffering.

### 2.  Identification with Jesus

When we suffer, we are identified with our Savior, the Suffering Servant. Martin Luther observed,

*Our suffering is not worthy of the name of suffering. When I consider my crosses, tribulations, and temptations, I shame myself almost to death; thinking what are they in comparison to the sufferings of my blessed Savior Christ Jesus.*[34]

One of the most unique aspects of Christianity is that God willingly took on our weakness, our pain, and our weeping. We serve a weeping Savior.

When we suffer, we are like our Savior and can be found in Him.

Paul keys in on this reality by saying,

*But we have this treasure in jars of clay to show that this all-surpassing power is from God and not from us. We are hard pressed on every side, but not crushed; perplexed, but not in despair; persecuted, but not abandoned; struck down, but not destroyed. We always carry around in our body the death of Jesus, so that the life of Jesus may also be revealed in our body.* (2 Cor. 4:7-10, NIV)

*For it has been granted to you that for the sake of Christ you should not only believe in him but also suffer for his sake. (Phil 1:29, ESV)*

When we suffer well, inviting the Holy Spirit to illuminate our perspective, we suffer knowing that just as our Savior suffered for us, so we suffer.

---

34   Martin Manser, ed., *Christian Quotations* (Martin Manser, 2016).

"

"There is a level of closeness to God that can only be accessed through pain and suffering."

"

### 3.    Produces Character

This is where the *hope* aspect really sets in. Unlike those who have not submitted to the Lordship of Christ, we know that God not only redeems pain but also uses pain to produce something in us. Our pain and suffering are not in vain when submitted to Jesus. God uses the trials and brokenness of a sin-infected world to refine and sanctify his kids. That is why James can say,

> *Consider it pure joy, my brothers and sisters, whenever you face trials of many kinds, because you know that the testing of your faith produces perseverance. Let perseverance finish its work so that you may be mature and complete, not lacking anything. (Jas 1:2-4, NIV)*

When submitted to Christ, trials test our faith and result in perseverance and maturity in our faith.

Similarly, Peter pens his first letter to those enduring intense persecution, a work widely believed to have been written during the reign of Nero. This emperor, as recorded by the Roman historian Tacitus, subjected Christians to horrific fates—feeding them to dogs, crucifying them, and even using their burning bodies as torches to illuminate his gardens.[35] So, suffice it to say, fidelity to Jesus was dangerous and suffering was inevitable. Yet, in this context, Peter records,

> *In all this you greatly rejoice, though now for a little while you may have had to suffer grief in all kinds of trials. These*

---

35    Tacitus, *Annals, 15.44.*

> *have come so that the proven genuineness of your faith—of greater worth than gold, which perishes even though refined by fire—may result in praise, glory, and honor when Jesus Christ is revealed. (1 Pet. 1:6-7, NIV)*

Peter, writing to a church facing martyrdom, encourages them to rejoice in their trials. Suffering and pain, when redeemed, test faith and are more valuable than gold. It results in something much more costly than a mortal, temporal life of ease; it has eternal ramifications.

When submitted to the Lordship of Jesus, suffering is *hopeful* because pain is not for nothing. Our suffering causes us to draw near to God, identify with the suffering of Jesus, and as our faith is tested in trial, spiritual gold—perseverance—is produced. Though God saves us, He does not pluck us out of the still broken, yet to be renewed world we are in. We have hope in suffering; something is being produced, *and* our suffering is temporary.

Pain is inevitable, yet temporary, and the disciple sets his gaze on the horizon, longing for the eternal. We will discuss this further in the following two chapters. To sum up this chapter, let the words of Paul sink in,

> *Therefore, we do not lose heart. Though outwardly we are wasting away, yet inwardly we are being renewed day by day. For our light and momentary troubles are achieving for us an eternal glory that far outweighs them all. So, we fix our eyes not on what is seen, but on what is unseen, since what is seen is temporary, but what is unseen is eternal. (2 Cor. 4:16-18, NIV)*

# chapter 6:
# the kingdom

_____

" *In Jesus Christ his followers have witnessed the Kingdom Of God breaking in on earth.*"

— *Dietrich Bonhoeffer*

Christians have their own language. Covered in the blood of the lamb. Propitiation. Sanctification. Nephilim.

Most Christians don't even know the meaning of our lingo. Often, phrases we sing, hands lifted, eyes shut, mind wandering, because we have no idea what meaning lies behind the words dancing off our lips. I would submit that one of the most used and least understood concepts in Christianity is the *Kingdom of God.* Yet, one scholar notes, "*According to the testimony of the first three Gospels, the proclamation of the kingdom of God was Jesus' central message.*"[36]

Simply put, I contend that most Christians misunderstand the central message of Jesus.

My favorite Gospel is Mark. The author is most frequently believed to be John Mark, mentioned in Acts, an associate of Paul and known in the early church as a disciple of Peter. In fact, most believe John Mark penned Peter's memories as he recounted the ministry of Jesus. The earliest known statement that confirms this sentiment comes from Papias in the late first or early second century. Kirk R. MacGregor suggests,

> *[Papias' statement] the earliest witness to Markan authorship. In his Interpretation of the Oracles of the Lord, Papias relates an earlier oral tradition (formulated ca. AD 80s) that Mark, though not an eyewitness, was Peter's interpreter in Rome*

---

36   George E. Ladd, "Kingdom of God (Heaven)," *Baker Encyclopedia of the Bible* (Grand Rapids, MI: Baker Book House, 1988), 1269.

> and *"wrote accurately, though not in order"* what Peter
> preached concerning *"the things said or done by the Lord.*[37]

Irenaeus carries the same tradition into the second century,

> *"Mark, the disciple and interpreter of Peter, did also hand
> down to us in writing what had been preached by Peter"*.

**Irenaeus** (2nd Century)

So, when we examine Mark, we likely find the earliest account of Jesus' ministry. Mark begins His account by asserting what he is setting out to demonstrate through narrative, *"The beginning of the good news about Jesus the Messiah, the Son of God."* (Mark 1:1, NIV) Every story chosen, every moment recorded, and every teaching collected is done to prove to the world that Jesus is *fully* God and *fully* man. With that in mind, let's observe the first words of Jesus in the first Gospel written.

> ... *Jesus came into Galilee, proclaiming the gospel of God, and saying, "The time is fulfilled, and the kingdom of God is at hand; repent and believe in the gospel."* (Mark 1:14-15, ESV)

Jesus begins His public ministry by proclaiming four things:

1. The Time is fulfilled

2. The Kingdom of God is at hand

3. Repent

4. Believe

---

37    Kirk R. MacGregor, "Mark, Gospel of," ed. John D. Barry et al., *The Lexham Bible Dictionary* (Bellingham, WA: Lexham Press, 2016).

Clearly, the Kingdom of God is a priority for Jesus. In fact, He uses the term *"Kingdom of God"* or *"Kingdom of Heaven"* over eighty times in the Gospels.

## Defining the Kingdom

So, let's get rid of the ambiguity. What is the Kingdom of God? Baker Encyclopedia of the Bible defines the Kingdom of God as,

> *The sovereign rule of God, initiated by Christ's earthly ministry and to be consummated when "the kingdom of the world has become the kingdom of our Lord and of his Christ.*[38]

In layman's terms, the Kingdom of God is *the rule and reign of God.*

Jesus came inaugurating the rule and reign of God. For Jesus' listeners, they would have been ecstatic. They were waiting for the literal, physical rule and reign of God. The Jewish people had gone from one oppressor to the next for thousands of years. Consider this: Egyptian rule lasted for 400 years, followed by a period of freedom under Moses and Joshua, then the Judges (a cycle of freedom to captivity), and finally relatively prosperous times between Samuel and the last of the kings. But then, it was Assyrian captivity for the ten lost tribes of Israel and Babylonian captivity for Judah. Followed by Persia and Greece, and now Rome. The Jews were *ready* for

---

38    George E. Ladd, "Kingdom of God (Heaven)," *Baker Encyclopedia of the Bible* (Grand Rapids, MI: Baker Book House, 1988), 1269.

God's physical Kingdom. They were prepared for the Romans to be overthrown and awaited the return of the Davidic kingdom's dominance.

This is where the problem comes in. The Jewish people were expecting physical liberation and their physical enemies to be overthrown. But that wasn't the phase of history they were living in; that wasn't the era of God's Kingdom that was being initiated. Jesus was overthrowing the *greatest* enemy to humanity: sin. Jesus was establishing His Kingdom covertly. He wasn't sending legions of angels to liberate the Jews physically; He, as the true King, was ushering in an era where the souls of men could be liberated from the tyranny of sin and death. Thus, many rejected Jesus' message. They wanted the temporal at the expense of the eternal.

I had a bible college professor explain the Kingdom of God with an illustration,

> *Picture a Kingdom brimming with formidable military power, vast strength, and abundant resources, invincible against any foe. Yet, within its borders, a faction rose in rebellion, turning away from the King's authority. The King holds the power to crush this uprising instantly, and one day, He will. For now, though, He permits it to persist out of love for the rebels, hoping as many as possible will recognize Him as the true King and abandon their revolt. His wish is for these rebels to gradually, one by one, recommit, re-enlist, and realign with His rule. Then, He intends to dispatch these reclaimed rebels back into the fray to infiltrate the rebellion and guide more souls home, one at a time.*

This is the Kingdom of God.

We are rebels who play a small part in the greater scheme of history. In His sovereign will, God has chosen to use former rebels as His voice box to help quell the rebellion. We are saved and regenerated when we see Jesus for who He is. Yet, He leaves us in the world, as broken and marred as it is, as insurgents, covert Kingdom operatives. We are on a mission for His Kingdom; our role is to see the ways of His Kingdom infiltrate the ways of this world. And part of the regeneration process initiated by the Holy Spirit's work in our lives is to realize that just as we were once rebels who have been welcomed in, now we must go, seek, search, and find other rebels, pleading with them to quit their rebellion and be united with their King.

## Monarchy

Before we move on to the theology behind the Kingdom, let's discuss monarchy. In the West, we lack a firm grasp of monarchy. We are the spawn of Enlightenment thinking. All of us are equal, and everyone's opinion carries equal weight. We fight for checks and balances. We are democratic, we have republics, and we have representatives. We vote, we have a say.

None of that is monarchical.

"

*"We are on a mission for His Kingdom; our role is to see the ways of His Kingdom infiltrate the ways of this world."*

"

For most of human history, there were monarchs. Kings and Queens ruled. In the West, our only real exposure is the United Kingdom. Which, though *technically* a monarchy, is not a traditional monarchy. It has been said that "*The British Monarchy is known as a constitutional monarchy. This means that, while The Sovereign is Head of State, the ability to make and pass legislation resides with an elected Parliament.*"[39] In a traditional monarchy, there is no parliament, no congress, no representatives or senators. What the sovereign says goes. They make the laws; they made the decisions. Their wish is command.

The Kingdom of God is a traditional monarchy. God is in control; what He says goes. The God who created all that we see not only has the right to determine how things go, but He also knows how everything functions *best*. When we respond to Jesus' invitation to follow Him, we are not only following Jesus, a Rabbi and teacher, but we are also transferring kingdoms; we have left the rebellion behind. We are stating with our actions that our priority is God's Kingdom. That is why Jesus teaches His disciples to pray,

> *Our Father in heaven,*
> *hallowed be your name.*
> *Your kingdom come,*
> *your will be done,*
> *on earth as it is in heaven.*

(Matt. 6:9-10, ESV)

---

39    "The Role of the Monarchy." The Royal Family. Accessed August 27, 2024. https://www.royal.uk/the-role-of-the-monarchy.

The heart of a disciple is to want God's rule and reign to expand, to grow, one heart, one person at a time. To follow Jesus is to have a heart that longingly declares, *"God, your Kingdom, your rule and reign come. Let your rule and reign expand on this planet. Let Earth look just like heaven."*

A follower of Jesus is about expanding God's Kingdom on earth. Grasping the nature of the Kingdom should cause us to cease chasing the fleeting joys of the temporary. We are agents dedicated to expanding freedom and hope on God's terms.

In other words, it is not about us.

We are a part of something bigger than ourselves.

Which gives us hope and purpose.

## Practical Implications of the Kingdom

The Kingdom of God is not only ever-expanding; it is deeply personal. Albert Schweitzer, who has been described as a French polymath, once opined, *"There can be no kingdom of God in the world without the kingdom of God in our hearts."*[40] The first place the rule and reign of God must be established is within the hearts and minds of followers of Jesus.

The Kingdom of God has personal implications.

Are *you* experiencing the rule and reign of God?

Has His Kingdom set up His rule and reign in *your* heart?

This personal aspect of His Kingdom is why Jesus continually preached about "inheriting" the Kingdom, or "entering" the

---

40    Albert Schweitzer, *An Anthology* (Boston: Beacon Press, 1956).

Kingdom. We have a part to play, and Paul warns about this aspect of God's Kingdom,

> *Or do you not know that the unrighteous will not inherit the kingdom of God? Do not be deceived: neither the sexually immoral, nor idolaters, nor adulterers, nor men who practice homosexuality, nor thieves, nor the greedy, nor drunkards, nor revilers, nor swindlers will inherit the kingdom of God.* (1 Corinthians 6:9, ESV)

> *Now the works of the flesh are evident: sexual immorality, impurity, sensuality, idolatry, sorcery, enmity, strife, jealousy, fits of anger, rivalries, dissensions, divisions, envy, drunkenness, orgies, and things like these. I warn you, as I warned you before, that those who do such things will not inherit the kingdom of God.* (Galatians 5:19-21, ESV)

> *…we exhorted each one of you and encouraged you and charged you to walk in a manner worthy of God, who calls you into his own kingdom and glory.* (1 Thessalonians 2:12, ESV)

Back to the illustration we used at the beginning, all of us are rebels; the question we must each answer is this:

*Have we left the rebellion and submitted to the leadership of the one true King?*

> *To want all that God wants, always to want it, for all occasions and without reservations, this is the kingdom of God which is all within.*

François Fénelon
(Archbishop of Cambrai)

So, the Kingdom of God is both vast and personal. Like most good theology, it is a grand paradox. As we wrap up this chapter, I want to explore three aspects of the Kingdom of God and dive into some theology.

## Theology of the Kingdom

When we talk about the Kingdom of God biblically, there are three aspects we need to consider.

### 1.    The Kingdom of God is eternal

The Kingdom of God is from eternity past to eternity future. Because God is eternal and has no beginning, His rule and reign have no beginning. He is and has always been in charge.

> *Your kingdom is an everlasting kingdom, and your dominion endures throughout all generations.* (Psalm 145:13, ESV)

> *The LORD will reign forever and ever.* (Exodus 15:18, ESV)

In Revelation, Jesus describes Himself,

> *"I am the Alpha and the Omega," says the Lord God, "who is and who was and who is to come, the Almighty."* (Revelation 1:8, ESV)

This verse describes the eternal nature of God and His Kingdom. There has never been a time when God was not in control. His Kingdom, His rule, and reign have always been the rule of the universe. Which brings hope. Regardless of what happens in my life, the good and the bad, I know who is ultimately in control. The world can go crazy, there can be conflicts across the globe, and pandemics raging, but over and above it all, there is a good God who not only has His hand on the pulse of history but directs it according to His will.

## 2. The Kingdom of God is now

This was the thrust of Jesus' teaching on the Kingdom. He repeatedly declared, "*The Kingdom is here, in your midst!*" Jesus was speaking to the reality that, in a tangible sense, *where the King is, His Kingdom is.* The rule and reign of God are here. It's not an ethereal or purely spiritual reality; it's tangible, accessible, and able to be tapped into and experienced. J.I. Packer wrote:

> *The task of the church is to make the invisible kingdom visible through faithful Christian living and witness-bearing… The church must make its message credible by manifesting the reality of kingdom life.*[41]

Following Jesus should practically manifest the rule and reign of God through our conduct.

Consider what happened when Jesus inaugurated this aspect of His Kingdom. Before the Sermon on the Mount, beginning with the Beatitudes in Matthew 5-8— perhaps the most extensive portrayal of *Kingdom Life*— Matthew highlights the potent force of the Kingdom that accompanied Jesus.

---

41    J.I. Packer, *Concise Theology: A Guide to Historic Christian Beliefs* (Carol Stream, IL: Tyndale House Publishers, 2001),194.

> *And he went throughout all Galilee, teaching in their synagogues*
> *and proclaiming the gospel of the kingdom and healing every*
> *disease and every affliction among the people. So his fame*
> *spread throughout all Syria, and they brought him all the sick,*
> *those afflicted with various diseases and pains, those oppressed*
> *by demons, those having seizures, and paralytics, and he healed*
> *them.* (Matthew 4:23-24, ESV)

As the Kingdom of God is proclaimed, its power becomes evident—healing the sick, driving out demons, and awakening those far off to the error of their ways.

Additionally, Jesus explained the Kingdom as an *invasion* of sorts. And this word *invasion* is essential. As we discussed in talking about suffering, our experience on this planet is a collision of two Kingdoms: The Kingdom of God and the Kingdom of Satan. Now, to be clear, this is not like a UFC fight where both sides are taking shots, and the results are in the air. We know who wins; there is no real battle here. Yet, God has sovereignly allowed a period of time for Satan to have a sphere of limited authority. To better understand the *now* aspect of the Kingdom, we must understand what Satan is doing.

### The Kingdom of Satan

There is a real God and there is a real devil. Satan is a Hebrew word that means "*adversary.*" Satan was an angel named Lucifer who was cast out of heaven. In the book of Isaiah, we find what is known as the "*Five I Wills of Satan.*" This is why he was cast out of heaven.

> *You said in your heart,*
> *'I will ascend to heaven;*
> *above the stars of God*
> *I will set my throne on high;*
> *I will sit on the mount of assembly*
> *in the far reaches of the north;*
> *I will ascend above the heights of the clouds;*
> *I will make myself like the Most High.'*

(Isaiah 14:13-14, ESV)

Ultimately, Lucifer tried to exalt himself; pride was the original sin. He briefly led a rebellion with a third of the angels, but just as quickly as they decided to rebel, God expelled them from His presence. Satan and his demonic forces have been granted a level of authority on this fallen, sinful world, temporarily. His goal on this planet is to thwart whatever God is doing.

> … *the god of this world has blinded the minds of the unbelievers, to keep them from seeing the light of the gospel of the glory of Christ, who is the image of God.* (2 Corinthians 4:4, ESV)

On this sinful, broken, rebellious planet, there is a king, a lower-case "g" god of this world that wants us to be sick, and broke, deceived, depressed, and blinded to the truth. That is the Kingdom of Darkness.

Yet, the '*now*' aspect of the Kingdom of God, the rule and reign of God, pushes back *that kingdom*. The sick are healed, the depressed find joy, the eyes of the blind are opened, we peer into the eternal; the eschatological end seeps through to the now.

*For the kingdom of God does not consist in talk but in power.*
(1 Corinthians 4:20, ESV)

*He has delivered us from the domain of darkness and transferred us to the kingdom of his beloved Son...*
(Colossians 1:13, ESV)

### 3. The Kingdom of God is not yet

God's dominion and reign endure forever, yet with Jesus' stepping onto the scene, a new era is inaugurated in which the kingdom of darkness can be tangibly overcome through the Holy Spirit's power, by the completed work of the Cross.

We can witness and participate in the power of the Kingdom. Yet, we still are affected by the consequences of sin. The effects of sin, Satan, and his demons are evident. But back to our illustration, there is a day when the King will quell the rebellion once and for all.

While we experience aspects of His Kingdom now, there are elements we don't see. There is still pain. Still sickness. Still disease. Still brokenness. Paul writes to the church in Corinth that at present, we see through a glass darkly. We catch glimpses of the Kingdom, but there will come a day when, like the unveiling of a masterpiece, we will see His Kingdom clearly.

The message throughout the New Testament to Christians facing hardship is the comforting assurance that their suffering is temporary and will ultimately give way to the full realization of God's Kingdom.

The apostolic writers encourage the church to live today in light of the *not yet* Kingdom of God. There will be a day when Jesus returns and establishes His Kingdom physically and eternally.

It is to that subject we now turn.

# chapter 7:
# back to the garden

———————

"…*between the death of Christ and the apostolic gospel of the cross there lay the resurrection, which alone gives the cross its redemptive power.*"

— *Dietrich Bonhoeffer*

When my wife and I first got married, I realized a terrible truth: she wasn't really into movies. She had never seen *Saving Private Ryan*, or *Gladiator*, or *Braveheart*, or *Indiana Jones*, or *Star Wars*.

True story: she didn't know who Harrison Ford was.

Selah.

I was nauseous for months after finding that out. I was distraught. I wept for her deprivation. Then, I discovered she had not seen one of my childhood favorites, *Hook*. This was too far.

I was disgusted.

Like any good husband, I forced her to watch it, chanting "*Rufio!*" as we went. To my dismay, she was not impressed.

*Hook* is an incredible ensemble of grown men playing fairytale characters. The beginning of the final battle between Robin Williams' *Peter Pan* and Dustin Hoffman's *Captain Hook* coincides with a beautiful exchange of dialogue,

> **Peter**: To die would be a great adventure.

> **Hook**: Death is the only adventure you have left.

In our opening chapter, we discussed spiritual death. Now, I want to talk about our physical death. More importantly, I want to zoom in and discuss what happens after death and even further down the road at the end of all things. Part of the reason disciples of Jesus have hope, maybe the greatest reason, is that we know how the story ends.

Before that, let's recap what we have covered so far:

Because of the finished work of the cross:

- *We have life*: regenerated, resuscitated by the power of the Holy Spirit.

- *We have hope*: life may come complete with suffering and pain, but not only will He produce something from our trials, but in the pain, we have a purpose, a Kingdom to advance, and that Kingdom, at the end, will be established for eternity.

Following Jesus is an ancient path to life and hope.

## Journey Back to Eden

There is a literary device the authors of Scripture often employed called an *inclusio*. In the realm of poetry, an *inclusio* has been defined as "*framing a poem by repeating words or phrases from its opening lines at its conclusion.*"[42] Inclusios are the sandwich effect; a saying, theme, or concept is repeated at the beginning and end of a literary work, and everything in the middle is to be interpreted through the lens of the repeated motif. *Inclusios* are evident not only in poetry but also throughout the Canon of Scripture to hammer home the author's point.

One example of this is seen in Matthew 19 and 20. In Matthew 19:30, Jesus says, "*But many who are first will be last,*

---

42   William W. Klein, Craig L. Blomberg, Robert L. Hubbard, Jr., (*Introduction to Biblical Interpretation,* (Nashville, TN: Thomas Nelson, INC, 2004), 303.

*and many who are last will be first."* (Matt. 19:30, NIV). He then proceeds to tell a parable about the Kingdom of Heaven. He likens the Kingdom to a landowner searching for workers to tend his vineyard. He hired workers at the beginning, middle, and end of the day. Yet, he paid them all the same. To emphasize His point, Jesus ends the parable with, *"So the last will be first, and the first will be last."* (Matt. 20:16, NIV)

I would argue that the Bible, from Genesis through Revelation, is an *inclusio.* It begins with God creating a world, void of sin, with His image bearers living in an unhindered relationship with their Creator. Then, Revelation ends with, *"Then I saw "'a new heaven and a new earth," for the first heaven and the first earth had passed away."* (Rev. 21:1, NIV)

John goes on to say,

> *I saw the Holy City, the new Jerusalem, coming down out of heaven from God, prepared as a bride beautifully dressed for her husband. And I heard a loud voice from the throne saying, "Look! God's dwelling place is now among the people, and he will dwell with them. They will be his people, and God himself will be with them and be their God. 'He will wipe every tear from their eyes. There will be no more death or mourning or crying or pain, for the old order of things has passed away.* (Rev.21:2-4, NIV)

Throughout all the bobbing and weaving of Scripture, a beautiful narrative arc emerges; all of Scripture describes a journey back to the Garden. From the foundations of the world, God, in His foreknowledge, knowing sin would infect

His creation, purposed to reestablish a *Garden City*. I am borrowing that language from John Mark Comer, who writes,

> *...most of the library of the New Testament is looking forward—to the Garden-like city. It's not about where we've come from as much as where we're going. It's almost like the New Testament writers are leaning forward with a pneumatic hope, stretching their neck out to see what's just over the horizon.*[43]

Yet, a challenge arises. Between Genesis 3, marking the Fall, and Revelation 21, heralding the New Heavens and New Earth, lies the reality of everyday life.

Life lies between the entrance of sin and ultimate restoration. As we have already discussed, life is full of pain and heartache. For Christians and non-believers alike, suffering awaits. Earth is broken, which means every system, every institution, our bodies, the weather, natural events, violence, the human psyche—all of it is broken.

The difference is *hope.*

For those who subscribe to some form of secular humanism, all the pain is for nothing. It is survival of the fittest.

The strong survive, the weak perish.

There is no purpose.

No redemption.

No reason.

---

43    John Mark Comer, *Garden City*, (Grand Rapids: Zondervan, 2015), 237.

No light at the end of the tunnel.

All that can be looked forward to is the day it all ends, and what we call *life* ceases.

As the Buddhists would say, *life is suffering.* Their goal is to reach *nirvana*, to cease to exist.

That's depressing.

For the Christian, there isn't just the possibility that pain and suffering will be redeemed—it's inevitable.

Death is actually the beginning of *true life.*

## Brand New

Throughout the New Testament, the various local churches are encouraged to remind themselves of God's ultimate purpose: the restoration of all things. Jesus speaks to this end in Revelation when He says, *"Behold, I am making all things new."* (Rev. 21:5, ESV)

In fact, through the power of Jesus and the infilling of the Holy Spirit, we see the first fruits of that newness now. Paul writes, *"...if anyone is in Christ, the new creation has come: The old has gone, the new is here!* (2 Cor. 5:17, NIV) Back to John Mark Comer, who comments on this verse, saying, *"So, new creation is here now; it's bursting through the cracks in the pavement, and it's starting with us."*[44]

I love the book of 2 Corinthians. Paul is in unique form as he addresses a church he loves dearly. Paul had a unique purpose in mind, as has been noted,

44    Comer, *Garden City,* 269.

*Paul wrote this follow-up letter to the church in Corinth to tell them how pleased he was that the people were sorry for the way they had acted and that they were now trying to live the way God wanted them to. He also defended himself against the accusations being made by false teachers.*[45]

Paul's prior letter to the Corinthian church was a rebuke; sexual immorality was everywhere, the services were a zoo, and they needed order and correction. History tells us the church received the rebuke with sincere hearts and made the necessary adjustments. Yet, some false apostles had infiltrated the church's ranks, casting doubt on the call of Paul and his associates. In addition to addressing various church matters, this letter is partly written to defend his apostolic call. Tucked between practical church instruction and his apostolic defense, Paul walks through doctrine on the resurrection. In this letter, we get some of the most beautiful verses in the Bible.

Relating to our purposes here, I want to zoom in on Paul's message of Christian hope. This book contains some of the most explicit reasons for Christians to have hope in all things. In Chapter 4, Paul outlines the pain and struggle, but also the hope that emerges through the process.

*Therefore we do not lose heart. Though outwardly we are wasting away, yet inwardly we are being renewed day by day. For our light and momentary troubles are achieving for us an eternal glory that far outweighs them all. So, we fix our eyes not on what is seen, but on what is unseen, since what is seen is temporary, but what is unseen is eternal.* (2 Cor. 4:16-18, NIV)

45   *The New International Version* (Grand Rapids, MI: Zondervan, 2011), 2 Co.

"For the Christian, there isn't just the possibility that pain and suffering will be redeemed—it's inevitable."

Paul urges the church to shift its focus from the present moment and fix its gaze on eternity. Or as one of my favorite protagonists would say,

*What we do in this life echoes in eternity.*

**Maximus Decimus Meridius,** *Gladiator*[46]

I want to spend the rest of this chapter breaking down the journey back to Eden and examining 2 Corinthians 5, as well as what we see in Revelation. I will make two distinctions that produce hope: *heaven* and the *New Heavens* and *New Earth.* Before we do, let's read this portion of Scripture,

> *For we know that if the earthly tent we live in is destroyed, we have a building from God, an eternal house in heaven, not built by human hands. Meanwhile we groan, longing to be clothed instead with our heavenly dwelling, because when we are clothed, we will not be found naked. For while we are in this tent, we groan and are burdened, because we do not wish to be unclothed but to be clothed instead with our heavenly dwelling, so that what is mortal may be swallowed up by life. Now the one who has fashioned us for this very purpose is God, who has given us the Spirit as a deposit, guaranteeing what is to come. Therefore we are always confident and know that as long as we are at home in the body we are away from the Lord. For we live by faith, not by sight. We are confident, I say, and would prefer to be away from the body and at home with the Lord. So we make it our*

---

46    Historically, this quote is often attributed to Marcus Aurelius though the exact phrase is not found in any of his writings.

*goal to please him, whether we are at home in the body or away from it. For we must all appear before the judgment seat of Christ, so that each of us may receive what is due us for the things done while in the body, whether good or bad.* (2 Cor. 5:1-10, NIV)

### 1. Heaven

Clouds.

Naked babies.

Harps.

Wings.

"*God gained an angel.*"

We have weird views about heaven. But are our ideas biblically accurate?

*Old Testament Heaven*

In the Old Testament, the term "heaven" has two distinct connotations. The first is associated with the physical cosmos. As Genesis 1 states, "*In the beginning God created the heavens and the earth.* (Gen.1:1, NIV) One scholar notes,

> *For the ancient Israelite, the cosmos consisted of heaven, earth, and the lower waters (Exod. 20:4). In the Hebrew Bible, heaven is the location of the clouds, the atmosphere (Job 35:5), and the area across which the stars journey in their paths (Jer. 8:2).* [47]

---

47  David Seal, "Heaven," ed. John D. Barry et al., *The Lexham Bible Dictionary* (Bellingham, WA: Lexham Press, 2016).

The basic idea is that *heaven* is what you see when you go outside and look up.

The second use of '*heaven*' in Scripture refers to the place where God dwells. The Hebrews saw a distinction between heaven and the *highest heaven*. The first is physical, the latter is God's dwelling. Solomon pulls from this idea when he declares, "*But will God indeed dwell on the earth? Behold, heaven and the highest heaven cannot contain you.*" (1 Kings 8:27, NIV) The ancients believed that God and the other celestial beings lived in a place that was *other*, higher than the earth.

For the earliest Jews, *heaven* was a place reserved for God and other heavenly beings, except for a few notable exceptions (e.g., Elijah, Enoch). Heaven was not a place you went when you died; it was reserved for the divine. The dead went to the realm of the dead, known as Sheol. It has been observed that "*Sheol as conceived in the OT [Old Testament] differs from the later doctrine of Hell in that it is the place where all the dead are gathered indiscriminately, both the good and the bad, the saints and the sinners.*"[48]

All who died found themselves "*gathered to their people.*" (Gen. 25:8, NIV) To reemphasize, Sheol was the destination for *all* who died, not just the wicked. But *heaven*, God's dwelling, was for God and God alone.

This is where there is a bit of separation. What happens after Sheol? Some Jews believed in a physical, bodily resurrection and the restoration of all things, while others did not. In fact,

---

48    Elwell and Barry J. Beitzel, "Sheol," *Baker Encyclopedia of the Bible*, 1948.

Jesus and Paul use this disagreement to their advantage in two instances. The Pharisees believed in the resurrection of the righteous, and the Sadducees did not.

> *That same day the Sadducees, who say there is no resurrection, came to him with a question.* (Matthew 22:23-45, NIV)

> *(The Sadducees say that there is no resurrection, and that there are neither angels nor spirits, but the Pharisees believe all these things.)* (Acts 23:8, NIV)

Josephus, who was a 1ˢᵗ-century Jewish historian speaking on the Pharisees' idea of death, recorded,

> *They also believe that souls have an immortal vigor in them, and that under the earth there will be rewards or punishments, according as they have lived virtuously or viciously in this life; and the latter are to be detained in an everlasting prison, but that the former shall have an easy return to life.*[49]

In another place, he wrote again of the Pharisees, "*They [the Pharisees] say that all souls are incorruptible, but that the souls of good men are only removed into other bodies, but that the souls of bad men are subject to eternal punishment.*"[50]

So, it seems the Pharisees had some concept of what we would call hell- defined as eternal, conscious torment- as punishment

---

49   Flavius Josephus, *Antiquities of the Jews*, 18.1.3.

50   Flavius Josephus, *The Jewish War*, 2.8.14.

for the wicked.[51] The wicked suffer eternal torment, and the righteous are resurrected to enjoy God's renewed creation.

The Pharisaical idea of resurrection was much closer to Christian thinking than that of the Sadducees.

### New Testament Heaven

When we delve into the New Testament, many of these ideas are carried over and expounded upon. Heaven is still used, from time to time, referring to the sky and cosmos.[52] Yet, the central perspective in the New Testament portrays heaven as the abode of God, from which Jesus came[53] and to which He has since ascended. In the most famous prayer in Scripture, Jesus begins with "*Our Father in heaven…*" (Matt. 6:9, NIV) Jesus also clearly states that His ascension was partly to "*…go to prepare a place for you…*" (Jn. 14:2, NIV) Jesus, expounding on the Old Testament idea of heaven being the dwelling place of God, seems to indicate that those who die in Christ will join God in that dwelling place.

This is the idea that Paul expounds on in 2 Corinthians 5,

> *For we know that if the earthly tent we live in is destroyed, we have a building from God, an eternal house in heaven, not built by human hands… We are confident, I say, and would prefer to be away from the body and at home with the Lord.* (2 Cor. 5:1,8, NIV)

---

51    For more on this see Appendix 1: Hell and Punishment

52    Matt. 6:26; Acts 2:19.

53    Jn 1:14, 18; Jn 3:13; 6:33-51; Heb. 4:14.

Paul indicates that when our earthly tent, our body, is destroyed, meaning we die, we enter into an eternal tent built by God. He then says that to be absent from the body is to be present with the Lord. According to Scripture, heaven is a spiritual place where believers go after death to be 1.) Absent from their physical body, and 2.) Be present with the Lord.

Another aspect of heaven is described in the book of Hebrews. The author describes the Old Testament tabernacles and temples as a shadow of what is happening in heaven, and Jesus Himself is the High Priest.

> *We do have such a high priest, who sat down at the right hand of the throne of the Majesty in heaven, and who serves in the sanctuary, the true tabernacle set up by the Lord, not by a mere human being... They serve at a sanctuary that is a copy and shadow of what is in heaven. (Heb. 8:1-2,5 NIV)*

The goal of the tabernacle system and the temple rituals was communion with God, though it was only a temporary solution. Through the finished work of the Cross, the temple system has come to an end; Jesus is our temple, Jesus is our High Priest, and Jesus is the initiator of the new covenant sealed in His blood. So, what is heaven in the New Testament?

> *Heaven is the spiritual reality believers step into after death, where God in His fullness dwells until the New Heavens and New Earth.*

This gives us hope. We have nothing to fear. If death comes, we enter God's unrestricted presence.

The reality of heaven gave early Christians, especially those facing persecution, unreasonable hope. The early church was odd to the prevailing culture for a number of reasons. One of which was how Christian death bordered on a cause for celebration within the Christian community. They constructed their places of worship around catacombs holding the remains of the martyrs. The bodies of those who had died for the Faith were carried in a spirit of celebration—death had been defanged. Church Father Athanasius wrote,

> *If you see children playing with a lion, don't you know that the lion must be either dead or completely powerless? In the same way...when you see Christ's believers playing with death and despising it, there can be no doubt that death has been destroyed by Christ and that its corruption has been dissolved and brought to an end.* [54]

### 2.  New Heavens and New Earth

So, heaven is the spiritual reality believers step into after death, where God, in His fullness, dwells until the New Heavens and New Earth. What do we mean by New Heavens and New Earth? Essentially, Jesus will return, and when He does, He will make *all things* new. The study of this period of time is known as *eschatology*, or the study of last things. There are varying views on exactly how the end plays out; my goal is not to discuss all those views here but to outline a few factors that all the eschatological views share.

---

54    Athanasius of Alexandria, *On the Incarnation*, 27.3. Translated by John Behr. Yonkers, NY: St. Vladimir's Seminary Press, 2011.

1. The Creation Renewed

Regardless of which eschatological camp one belongs to, we all agree that this world will be destroyed, and a new one will come. With the entrance of sin came brokenness of the literal, physical planet. God said in Genesis, "...*Cursed is the ground because of you...*" (Gen.3:17b, NIV). From Genesis 3 on, the theme of the earth being temporary is explicit,

> *See, the LORD is going to lay waste the earth and devastate it;*
>
> *he will ruin its face... The earth will be completely laid waste*
>
> *and totally plundered. The LORD has spoken this word. The*
>
> *earth dries up and withers, the world languishes and withers*
> (Is. 24:1, 3-4, NIV)
>
> *...The heavens will disappear with a roar; the elements will*
> *be destroyed by fire, and the earth and everything done in it*
> *will be laid bare... That day will bring about the destruction*
> *of the heavens by fire, and the elements will melt in the heat.*
> (2 Pet. 3:10, 12, NIV)
>
> *Heaven and earth will pass away, but my words will never*
> *pass away.* (Matt. 24:35, NIV)
>
> *In the beginning, Lord, you laid the foundations of the earth,*
>
> *and the heavens are the work of your hands.*
>
> *They will perish, but you remain;*
>
> *they will all wear out like a garment.*
>
> *You will roll them up like a robe;*
>
> *like a garment they will be changed.*

*But you remain the same,*

*and your years will never end.* (Heb. 1:10-12, NIV)

This physical world will be done away with, and the consequences of sin will be destroyed. God's plan after the destruction of the planet is the recreation of a sinless world, and with it, those who are redeemed will be resurrected to eternal, embodied life with Jesus.

## 2.    Resurrection of the dead

The spiritual reality known as heaven is not the same thing as the renewed creation. The Doctrine of Resurrection begins with Jesus' resurrection. When Jesus was resurrected, there was physicality to it. The disciples touched his body, the holes in his hands, feet, and side. He ate, and He walked the Road to Emmaus. Now, Jesus evidently walked through a locked door, suggesting some significant differences between temporal and resurrected bodies. However, just as Christ was physically raised from the dead, the New Testament clearly teaches that Jesus' disciples will also be raised.

Paul discusses this in 1 Corinthians 15. Here, I quote Paul at length to gain a deeper understanding of the theology of resurrection. So, we will read a little bit and comment a little bit as we work through this passage.

*But if it is preached that Christ has been raised from the dead, how can some of you say that there is no resurrection of the dead? If there is no resurrection of the dead, then not even Christ has been raised. And if Christ has not been raised, our preaching is useless and so is your faith. More than that, we are then found to be false witnesses about God, for we have testified about God that he raised Christ from the dead. But he did not raise him if in fact the dead are not raised. For if the dead are not raised, then Christ has not been raised either. And if Christ has not been raised, your faith is futile; you are still in your sins. Then those also who have fallen asleep in Christ are lost. If only for this life we have hope in Christ, we are of all people most to be pitied.* (1 Cor. 15:12-19, NIV)

Paul teaches that the resurrection of the saints is tethered to Jesus' bodily resurrection. If He was resurrected, then so will we. If He wasn't resurrected, we are still guilty of our sins, and hell awaits. Starting in v.20, Paul argues that Christ was raised from the dead and was the first of the "New Creation," the "first fruits". Just as sin and death entered through Adam, so Jesus, as the *Second Adam*, brings life. He continues to argue for the resurrection of our earthly body while distinguishing between what is mortal and what is eternal. Then, in verse 42, he explains what we can expect on the last day.

*So will it be with the resurrection of the dead. The body that is sown is perishable, it is raised imperishable; it is sown in dishonor, it is raised in glory; it is sown in weakness, it is raised in power; it is sown a natural body, it is raised a spiritual body. If there is a natural body, there is also a spiritual body. So, it is written: "The first man Adam became a living being"; the last Adam, a life-giving spirit. The spiritual did not come first, but the natural, and after that the spiritual. The first man was of the dust of the earth; the second man is of heaven. As was the earthly man, so are those who are of the earth; and as is the heavenly man, so also are those who are of heaven. And just as we have borne the image of the earthly man, so shall we bear the image of the heavenly man. I declare to you, brothers and sisters, that flesh and blood cannot inherit the kingdom of God, nor does the perishable inherit the imperishable. Listen, I tell you a mystery: We will not all sleep, but we will all be changed—in a flash, in the twinkling of an eye, at the last trumpet. For the trumpet will sound, the dead will be raised imperishable, and we will be changed. For the perishable must clothe itself with the imperishable, and the mortal with immortality. When the perishable has been clothed with the imperishable, and the mortal with immortality, then the saying that is written will come true: "Death has been swallowed up in victory."*

*"Where, O death, is your victory?*

*Where, O death, is your sting?"*

*The sting of death is sin, and the power of sin is the law. But thanks be to God! He gives us the victory through our Lord Jesus Christ.* (1 Cor. 15:42-57, NIV)

Part of Christian hope is linked to our physical, literal, embodied resurrection. Our broken, sin-marred bodies will be renewed to a glorified state in the manner of Jesus' glorified body. At that time, those who are in Christ will enjoy an unhindered relationship with their Creator on a sinless, perfect planet for eternity. Resurrection is coming, one day.

### 3.    It will be unexpected

One of my pet peeves is the class of Christians I affectionately call "*Coming of Jesus Predictors.*" They drive me insane. Every few years, a video will go viral, or a new book will be released "revealing" the exact moment of the Second Coming. These magicians have correctly dissected the text, added up the blood moons and red Heffers, and cracked the code.

2012 anyone?

There is a massive problem with this: the words of Jesus. Jesus Himself said,

> *But concerning that day and hour no one knows, not even the angels of heaven, nor the Son, but the Father only.* (Matt. 24:36, ESV)

Matthew 24 is all about what the end of time will look like. Earthquakes, famines, wars, and rumors of wars. He explains that He is going to literally, physically, split the clouds with the sound of a trumpet, and all will see Jesus, who came as the Lamb of God the first time, but He will return as the Lion of Judah to judge the living and the dead. It's an epic description. But, as far as timing goes, Jesus says *only* the Father knows when this will happen.

Jesus is going to come back; that much is certain. What is just as certain is that it will be unexpected. Jesus tells a parable about ten virgins waiting for the groomsman. In the meantime, they ran out of oil and missed His arrival. The moral of the story is to stay ready; you don't know when He is going to return.

Paul expounds on this idea, saying,

> *Now, brothers and sisters, about times and dates we do not need to write to you, for you know very well that the day of the Lord will come like a thief in the night. While people are saying, "Peace and safety," destruction will come on them suddenly, as labor pains on a pregnant woman, and they will not escape. But you, brothers and sisters, are not in darkness so that this day should surprise you like a thief. You are all children of the light and children of the day. We do not belong to the night or to the darkness. So then, let us not be like others, who are asleep, but let us be awake and sober* (1 Thess. 5:1-6, NIV)

Paul describes Jesus' second coming as a thief in the night, a time when most people are caught sleeping. He encourages the church to stay awake and live today as if Jesus is returning tomorrow.

Peter urges the same thing,

> *But the day of the Lord will come like a thief, and then the heavens will pass away with a roar, and the heavenly bodies will be burned up and dissolved, and the earth and the works that are done on it will be exposed. Since all these things are thus to be dissolved, what sort of people ought you to be in lives of holiness and godliness, waiting for and hastening the coming of the day of God, because of which the*

> *heavens will be set on fire and dissolved, and the heavenly*
> *bodies will melt as they burn! But according to his promise*
> *we are waiting for new heavens and a new earth in which*
> *righteousness dwells. (2 Peter 3:10-13, ESV)*

Jesus' return will come suddenly. There are signs, but no one can predict exactly when this will happen. In light of the age to come, we live differently. We live holy, righteous lives, looking to be found spotless before the King and longing to hear, "*Well done, good and faithful servant,*" from our Master.

We will elaborate on what this looks like in practice in *Part 3: Flourishing.*

## Conclusion

When we consider what it means to follow Jesus, it begins with our inescapable need for salvation. Following Jesus begins when we recognize that we need *life.* Life comes from the power of the Holy Spirit, and *hope* comes with Him. This world is broken, marred by sin, suffering, and pain are inevitable. But our suffering is not trivial; it's productive, and we suffer with purpose, knowing we live to advance an eternal Kingdom and that one day, that Kingdom, though presently invisible, will be established literally, physically, and eternally in the New Heavens and the New Earth.

Until that time, we long for Jesus to come. Our souls crave our homeland; we are dual citizens, though our true motherland is not of this world. We seek to advance the purposes of God on this side of eternity while inwardly yearning to experience the next. If Jesus tarries, and His second coming is delayed by another two millennia, we die in hope, being joined to the spiritual reality of heaven, where God dwells in His fullness. So, we have *hope.*

*Hope* in the here.

*Hope* in the now.

*Hope* that in the end, God will make everything right. Our souls groan for Jesus to come; we know *"This ain't it."* Jesus will return, and if I die before that happens, I will see Him face-to-face in paradise.

N.T. Wright explains this idea by writing, *"…the one who is presently in heaven will come back and transform the earth, where we have lived as a colonial outpost of heaven waiting for that day."* [55]

We conclude this section with Paul's words. I encourage you to read this text slowly, contemplate deeply, and hope eternally.

> *But our citizenship is in heaven. And we eagerly await a Savior from there, the Lord Jesus Christ, who, by the power that enables him to bring everything under his control, will transform our lowly bodies so that they will be like his glorious body. (Phil. 3:20-21, NIV*

---

55    N.T Wright, *Paul,* (London: First Fortress Press, 2009), 143.

part 3:

# flourishing

*Flourishing is defined as 'developing rapidly and successfully; thriving.' Flourishing is about thriving in the here and now—in this life—in this moment. This book outlines discipleship in a three-step process, prioritizing each step in order of importance.*

> **Life** – *We are dead in sin, and only in Christ can we be brought to life.*

> **Hope** – *This planet is still broken, and we need something to set our sights on.*

> **Flourishing** – *In the here and now, we can thrive.*

*Our modern ethos reverses this order. Flourishing is the apple of the eye of culture; God exists to enhance my right now. I contend that God does care about your right now, but not as much as your spiritual deadness, and giving you hope by fixing your eyes on His grand scheme for eternity. In this section, we explore what flourishing looks like for those who follow Jesus. But I will spill the beans now and say, in short, flourishing happens when we live according to God's design.*

# chapter 8:
# under the mask

---

*"Christians are no longer to be called sinners... On the contrary, they were once sinners, ungodly, enemies... but now through Christ they are holy. As saints they are reminded and exhorted to be what they are."*

**— Dietrich Bonhoeffer**

I have an unhealthy obsession with Spider-Man. As did my father before me. My dad was born in 1956 and started collecting comics as soon as they were available. My dad is a purist when it comes to comics; if it didn't come from the 60s, to him, it's not canon, regardless of what the MCU says. Growing up, we went to comic bookstores and *Toys 'R' Us* looking for anything with the wall-crawler on it. This obsession ended with Spidey's face tattooed on my back.

Whenever I dive into comics or watch movies packed with vigilantes, I'm always struck by how no one seems able to uncover the true identities of these superheroes.

How does Superman put on glasses and confuse the world?

How can no one put two and two together that Peter Parker and Spider-Man are never in the same place at the same time?

How does no one find the Batcave?

Serious questions for a serious time.

In the context of discipleship, Christians possess a kind of secret identity. However, it's not that believers are intentionally keeping it hidden—most aren't aware it exists at all. Put more plainly, too many Christians *do not know who they really are.*

Christian flourishing begins with identity.

Life flows from who you are.

The inquiry into human identity has been one of the most intensely contested subjects throughout history. What makes me *me?* Is it simply atoms, neurons, and protons? Is it just matter? Or is there an essence? A soul? A spirit? What is humanity? Are we simply higher primates whose knuckle-dragging has gone the proverbial way of the buffalo?

## Philosophical Underpinnings

France has always been a land of thinkers and philosophy.

Rene Descartes.

Jean-Jacques Rousseau.

Jean-Paul Sartre.

Michel Foucault.

Jacques Derrida.

Most of them had horrific ideas. Horrifically profound.

Rene Descartes was obsessed with the idea of existence and pondered the question, *"How can we prove anything is real?"* After much reflection, he concluded that the very fact that he could reflect meant he existed. This revelation spawned the famous phrase,

*Cogito, ergo sum*

*I think, therefore I am.*

He located the epicenter of identity in the psychological realm. Bringing us back to, "I *am what happens between my ears*." While his diagnosis may contain some truth, it's clear that the story of identity goes beyond just what we think and feel. Descartes lived in the 17th century; our captivation with existence has only intensified over the past four centuries.

**"**

*"Christian flourishing begins
with identity."*

**"**

This chapter is about Christian identity. It is about who we are through the lens, the framework, of the finished work of the Cross.

## Imago Dei

All good theology originates in Genesis. To reemphasize what was stated in the intro,

*Flourishing occurs when we live according to God's design.*

To find the most explicit definition of that design, let's look at the creation of man.

In the beginning, God began His work of Creation. He spoke light, vegetation, and wildlife into existence. Then, it appears that the Godhead has a conversation about creating an image bearer, one who will expand the franchise and be the head of the created order.

> *Let us make mankind in our image in our likeness, so that they may rule over the fish in the sea and the birds in the sky, over the livestock and all the wild animals, and over all the creatures that move along the ground. So God created mankind in his own image, in the image of God he created them; male and female he created them.* (Gen. 1:26-27, NIV)

Man was different from the rest of creation. Genesis 2 zooms in on God's creative process,

> *God blessed them and said to them, "Be fruitful and increase in number; fill the earth and subdue it. Rule over the fish in the sea and the birds in the sky and over every living creature that moves on the ground.* (Gen. 1:28, NIV)

First, notice the intentionality present in the formation of man. In the creation of man, God formed and breathed. He spent time shaping and molding this image bearer. Not only is time devoted to the forming process, but after the forming process, God speaks directly to the man and woman, giving them purpose. From this first snapshot of humanity, we see that God spent time *on* them and God spent time *with* them. The first humans were created to hear God's voice and be near Him.

Genesis 2 contains a verse that is often overlooked or misconstrued. God brings Eve to Adam, and in doing so, gives humanity the gift of marriage. Marriage serves to illustrate God's covenant love for His people, and God Himself presided over that first marriage. Adam, upon seeing his wife, sings a love song, and the Bible records a beautiful detail, "*Adam and his wife were both naked, and they felt no shame.*" (Gen. 2:25, NIV)

In the beginning, when God created humanity, He created them in His image (we will explore this in a moment), gave them a purpose for life, and united them together in such beautiful matrimony that love songs burst forth. Shame is absent; Adam and Eve were fully secure in their nakedness.

Sin has corrupted every element of design we just explored. When Adam and Eve disobey God and eat the forbidden fruit, a few things happen:

- *They see their nakedness-* They are no longer naked and unashamed. Shame has entered the chat.

- *They hide from God-* Their relationship with the purpose-giver is estranged. Sin causes separation, and they are ultimately removed from the garden.

- *They blame each other* - Humanity's interrelated, interconnected blueprint is in jeopardy.

All of that has to do with design and identity. Interestingly enough, those elements destroyed by sin were reconstructed by Jesus on the Cross. So, let's break these down one at a time.

## Shame on you

Guilt and shame are not the same thing. Guilt is good; it is God's moral law tugging on our hearts, pulling us towards morality. Shame is a different animal altogether.

Shame nags.

Shame destroys.

Shame distorts the *Imago Dei.*

Before we define shame, let's look at what it means to be the *Imago Dei.* Imago Dei means *Image of God* in Latin. God made us in His image. Most of us have heard that phrase, but what does it mean?

Recently, a statue was unveiled in honor of the late Kobe Bryant and his daughter, Gianna "Gigi" Bryant. The sculpture depicts Kobe with his arm around Gigi, an inscription lies below featuring a quote of his that ends with the phrase, "*I'm a girl dad.*" Gazing at that statue, you're reminded of a father who placed his children first, dedicating himself fully to nurturing their talents.

The image of Kobe and the inscription therein cause you to reflect on the greatness of the man.

When you look at the statue of Kobe, you think about Kobe; you don't reflect on the wonder of the bronze, the material the statue is made of. The image is intended to remind viewers of the greatness of the one it depicts.

The same is true of us; we are images. Our job is not to absorb glory but to reflect it. When people see our lives, they should reflect on the goodness of God.

The Imago Dei in us does a few things:

### 1.    Differentiates us from God

God is the One whose image *we bear*. We are not God, and it is good to be clear that *He* is God, and we are not.

### 2.    Elevates humanity about animals

Only man was made in God's image. Although we are responsible for cultivating and caring for this planet, including the animal kingdom, we are worth more than animals. We are not animals; we are image-bearers.

### 3.    Image bearing implies inherent value and worth

The occupation of reflecting the nature and glory of God to all creation necessitates value due to our uniqueness among God's created order. When we live as we should, others should catch a faint reflection of God in us.

In the 2nd century, St. Irenaeus said, "*The glory of God is a living man, and the life of man consists in beholding God.*"[56] Though only a fraction, the glory of God should be revealed in humanity, and, above all, our goal should be to behold God.

So, we are made in His image, yet the entrance of sin marred that image. The image is still there, but sin put some rust on it. St. Augustine hints at this and God's redemptive power, writing, "*The image of God has been deformed by sin, but it can be reformed in the soul by God's grace.*"[57] St. Ambrose addresses this same concept: "*Sin, like a disease, corrupts the image of God in man. But the medicine of grace heals and restores us to our former dignity.*"[58]

The concept of identity—and the belief that our lives flow from our true selves—ultimately centers on the restoration of the *Imago Dei*, a return to Eden.

Now, let's get back to shame. Biblically, shame is defined as "*Feelings associated with (but not limited to) failure, public*

---

56    St. Irenaeus, *Against Heresies*, Book IV, Chapter 20, Section 7, in *Ante-Nicene Fathers*, ed. Alexander Roberts and James Donaldson, trans. A. Cleveland Coxe (Buffalo, NY: Christian Literature Publishing Co., 1885), reprinted in *The Early Church Fathers* series.

57    St. Augustine, *On the Trinity*, Book XIV, Chapter 15, in *The Nicene and Post-Nicene Fathers*, First Series, Vol. 3, ed. Philip Schaff, trans. Arthur West Haddan (Buffalo, NY: Christian Literature Publishing Co., 1887), reprinted in *The Early Church Fathers* series.

58    St. Ambrose, *On the Duties of the Clergy*, Book I, Chapter 13, in *Nicene and Post-Nicene Fathers*, Second Series, Vol. 10, ed. Philip Schaff and Henry Wace, trans. H. De Romestin (Buffalo, NY: Christian Literature Publishing Co., 1896), reprinted in *The Early Church Fathers* series.

*exposure, disgrace, embarrassment, social rejection, ridicule, and dishonor."* [59]

Shame played a significant cultural role in both the Ancient Near East and Western societies. In Greece, shame served to keep individuals aligned with the public's interests. Shame encouraged individuals to live dignified lives; acceptance and respect were contingent upon proper conduct. There were rules to human interaction; shame resulted from living in opposition to the agreed-upon terms of social cohesion. A shameless person disregarded these rules.[60] The Bible reflects this honor-shame society in punishments for wrongdoing, a pattern clearly demonstrated in the behavior of war victors, with the aim of instilling shame in the guilty party.

> *Techniques such as enemies being thrown at the feet of the victor were aimed at bringing dishonor or shame on the person. For example, Joshua orders his captains to "put [their] feet on the necks" of the defeated kings (Josh 10:24). This gesture provides a public display of physical dominance.*[61]

Living a life free of shame was of utmost importance.

In modern times, shame has largely been regarded as a harmful force within secular psychology. Research shows that shame can lead to avoidance of relationships and vulnerability,

---

59    David Seal, "Shame," ed. John D. Barry et al., *The Lexham Bible Dictionary* (Bellingham, WA: Lexham Press, 2016).

60    Malina, Bruce J. *The New Testament World: Insights from Cultural Anthropology.* Louisville, KY.: Westminster John Knox, 1981.

61    Matthews, Victor H. "Making Your Point: The Use of Gestures in Ancient Israel." *Biblical Theology Bulletin* 42 (2012): 18–29.

emotional suppression, mental health challenges, hesitation to take risks, relapse, and addiction.[62]

Brene Brown, a research professor and TED Talk lecturer, has extensively studied the effects of shame. She states, "*Shame corrodes the very part of us that believes we are capable of change.*"[63]

Shame holds us captive to our past.

Shame reminds us of the folly of yesterday.

Shame declares, "*THAT* is who you are and will forever be."

Yet, through the finished work of the Cross, the journey back to the Garden is available. To be naked and unashamed. To be known and loved. To have nothing to hide because all is forgiven, *that* is true flourishing.

And *that* is part of the provision of the Cross.

In the Gospel of Luke, we get an epic snapshot of Jesus articulating who He is and what His mission is. Jesus had just wrapped up a forty-day fast in the wilderness where He defeated Satan, and He returns in the "*power of the Holy Spirit.*" (Luke 4:14) Shortly after, Jesus steps into a synagogue and opens the scroll to Isaiah 61 and reads,

> *The Spirit of the Lord is on me,*
>
> *because he has anointed me*

---

62    Clearview Treatment Programs, "*The Effects of Shame on Mental Health and Addiction Recovery*," Clearview Treatment, accessed September 2024, https://www.clearviewtreatment.com.

63    Brené Brown, *Daring Greatly: How the Courage to Be Vulnerable Transforms the Way We Live, Love, Parent, and Lead* (New York: Gotham Books, 2012), 73.

*to proclaim good news to the poor.*

*He has sent me to proclaim freedom for the prisoners*

*and recovery of sight for the blind,*

*to set the oppressed free,*

*to proclaim the year of the Lord's favor."*

*Then he rolled up the scroll, gave it back to the attendant and sat down. The eyes of everyone in the synagogue were fastened on him. He began by saying to them, "Today this scripture is fulfilled in your hearing." (Luke 4:18-21, NIV)*

Isaiah 61 goes into more detail explaining what this messianic figure would do,

*Instead of your shame*

*you will receive a double portion,*

*and instead of disgrace*

*you will rejoice in your inheritance.*

*And so you will inherit a double portion in your land,*

*and everlasting joy will be yours.* (Is. 61:7, NIV)

Jesus throws the gauntlet, "*I AM the fulfillment of this 500-year-old prophecy.*" His mission is clear, His method apparent. Part of the fulfillment of this text, which Jesus clearly states has come, is that shame would be exchanged for favor.

Scripture is replete with the idea of shame being removed from us and placed onto Jesus at Calvary. In Romans, after indicating the method of salvation as confession and belief,

Paul quotes Isaiah: "*Anyone who believes in him will never be put to shame*" (Rom. 10:11, NIV). Peter quotes this same verse in 1 Peter 2:6.

At the cross, the chains of the past, the exposing of our nakedness, are done away with. We live through the lens of 2 Corinthians 5:17,

> *Therefore, if anyone is in Christ, the new creation has come: The old has gone, the new is here! All this is from God, who reconciled us to himself through Christ and gave us the ministry of reconciliation: that God was reconciling the world to himself in Christ, not counting people's sins against them.* (2 Cor. 5:17-19a, NIV)

The cross of Jesus made us new by removing our sin, and He struck a death blow to our shame by taking it upon Himself. In other words, through the cross of Christ, we can be naked and unashamed. A road to Eden is restored, and shamelessness is a significant component of our renewed identity and our flourishing in this life.

## Hide and Seek

In addition to the removal of our shame, a path has been forged to restore humanity's connection with its Creator.

Back to Genesis, after sin, shame shows up, and Adam and Eve hide from God. The entrance of sin forms a relational gap between man and God.

We often speed past the sin of Adam and Eve due to familiarity.

*"Ya, ya, I know the story."*

But let's slow down and read,

> *Then the man and his wife heard the sound of the LORD God as he was walking in the garden in the cool of the day, and they hid from the LORD God among the trees of the garden.* (Gen. 3:8, NIV)

Adam and Eve hide after hearing God *walk* through the Garden, which seems to suggest that God walking in the Garden was a regular occurrence. Prior to sin, humanity ran around butt-naked with its Creator there, face-to-face. Then sin happens, bringing shame and causing man to fear God. That fear stems from a deeper, spiritual reality.

The prophet Isaiah lays this out,

> *But your iniquities have separated*
> *you from your God;*
> *your sins have hidden his face from you,*
> *so that he will not hear.* (Is. 59:2, NIV)

Sin separates humanity from God.

Fear and estrangement replace love and connection.

In the end, sin results in a void, a profound sense of emptiness, a deep knowing that the human experience, in and of itself, is incomplete.

## The Human Experience

Growing up in the 1990s was awesome. I know Gen.X believes the '80s were the greatest, and they are entitled to their incorrect opinion. '90s cinema is unmatched: Jurassic Park, Saving Private Ryan, and Braveheart. That's not to mention the comedies and Disney classics—the golden age.

Two particular stars ruled the silver screen: Robin Williams and Jim Carrey. Robin Williams starred as Peter Pan, *Mrs. Doubtfire*, and the Genie from *Aladdin*. Robin Williams is arguably one of the most talented actors and comedians of the last 50 years. Yet, even with success and stardom, Williams struggled with depression. Though rarely talking about his pain, he is credited with saying, "*I think the saddest people always try their hardest to make people happy. Because they know what it feels like to feel absolutely worthless, and they don't want anybody else to feel like that.*" I will never forget the day I heard the news that Robin Williams, the comedian, the Genie, the goof from Flubber, took his own life in 2014.

Jim Carrey, another eccentric comedian who starred in *The Mask* and *Ace Ventura,* alludes to the same theme, saying, "*I think everybody should get rich and famous and do everything they ever dreamed of so they can see that it's not the answer.*"[64]

I would argue that these celebrities are expressing, though unknowingly, what the writer of Ecclesiastes declared around the 10th century BC: "*He has also set eternity in the human heart*" (Ecc. 3:11, NIV). At the core of humanity, there is a deep knowing that there is more than *this*. That *more* is the human longing, the human cry for connection with its Creator.

---

64    Jim Carrey, interview with Jay Stone, 2005, as cited in *AZ Quotes*, accessed September 2024, https://www.azquotes.com/quote/520133.

In the 4th century, St. Gregory of Nyssa wrote, "*The soul, created to seek and love the Beautiful, yearns unceasingly for the beauty of the divine, since it was made to reflect that beauty.*"[65]

17th-century mathematician and scientist, Blaise Pascal, was deeply skeptical of a personal God. He preferred the plane of numbers, equations, and empirical evidence. That is, until what he called the *Night of Fire*. That night, he came face to face with his Creator, and as he describes,

> "*Fire. God of Abraham, God of Isaac, God of Jacob, not of the philosophers and scholars. Certitude. Certitude. Feeling. Joy. Peace. God of Jesus Christ. Thy God shall be my God. Forgetfulness of the world and of everything, except God. He is only found by the ways taught in the Gospel. Grandeur of the human soul. Righteous Father, the world has not known thee, but I have known thee. Joy, joy, joy, tears of joy.*"[66]

The skeptic had a personal encounter with his Creator.

After this moment, Blaise often wore a jacket with a document sewn into its lining called his *"Memorial."* This document held his thoughts and feelings about the *Night of Fire*.

He encountered a God who is not an intellectual *idea* but an experiential *person*—*a* God who loves humanity and *wants* to be known. Sin created a chasm, but Jesus bridged the divide.

---

65  St. Gregory of Nyssa, *The Life of Moses*, Book II, in *The Classics of Western Spirituality* series, trans. Abraham J. Malherbe and Everett Ferguson (New York: Paulist Press, 1978), 86.

66  Blaise Pascal, *Memorial*, trans. W. F. Trotter, in *Pensées*, ed. A.J. Krailsheimer (New York: Penguin Classics, 1966), 309-310.

At the heart of our identity as followers of Jesus lies one of the most essential qualities: our pursuit of God.

The author of Hebrews, after explaining all that Jesus has done, lays out how we are to respond to His sacrifice and what is available because of it.

> *Therefore, since we have a great high priest who has ascended into heaven, Jesus the Son of God, let us hold firmly to the faith we profess For we do not have a high priest who is unable to empathize with our weaknesses, but we have one who has been tempted in every way, just as we are—yet he did not sin. Let us then approach God's throne of grace with confidence, so that we may receive mercy and find grace to help us in our time of need.* (Heb. 4:14-16, NIV)

The gap seen in Eden after sin, Adam and Eve hiding from God, has been done away with. Intimacy has been restored. God is walking in the cool of the day, and there is an invitation for Man to know[67] and be known by his Creator.

When we speak of our identity in Christ, specifically in tandem with an Edenic restoration, our renewed identity in Christ has removed our shame and restored our relationship with God. Though we experience both of those restorations imperfectly on this side of eternity, we will see their *full* restoration one day.

---

67  When we talk about knowing God, it's important to emphasize that we can only know what God has revealed in Scripture. God is bigger and greater than our finite minds can comprehend. We cannot comprehensively know God, but God has revealed who He is in ways we can comprehend.

## Not My Brother's Keeper

The third Edenic element connected to Christian identity that finds restoration is a renewal of human connection. We all need people, yet in the hyper-individualistic culture of 21st-century America, many Christians misunderstand the vital importance of meaningful human connection.

*"I have church on my boat."*

*"Me, Jesus, a fishing pole, and a beer."*

*"All I need is Jesus."*

Ya, that's not true.

Let's go back to Genesis.

God creates everything, and all of it is good. Trees, good. Skies, good. Oceans, good. Man, very good. Note the environment Adam is in. Adam lives in a sinless garden; God takes morning walks amongst Eden's lilies.

Just Adam, God, and the animals.

The good life.

Yet, in that very environment, God makes a statement, *"It is not good for the man to be alone. I will make a helper suitable for him."* (Gen. 2:18, NIV)

Even though Adam is in a sinless, optimal environment, just him and His God, God declares, *"not good."* This seems to indicate that from the beginning, from our *design*, we need the company of other image bearers.

As Genesis 3 unfolds, the consequences of sin emerge with the entrance of shame, Adam and Eve being gripped by fear as they hide from God, and a wedge being driven between them as the blame-shifting starts. Blame shifting quickly turns to murder, and strife, and war, and abuse, and exploitation.

The result of sin is a separation not only between God and man but also between man and man. Due to our design, we cannot flourish in isolation. So, what do we do?

## God's People

One of the most fascinating aspects of God's humanity-saving strategy is His process for selecting leaders. Throughout the biblical narrative, God chooses brash, degenerate, broken vessels to bring about His righteous purposes.

Consider the founding of God's covenant people, Israel. God chooses a man, Abraham, who has his own plethora of shortcomings. Yet, this man's lineage becomes the nation of Israel. Israel goes through repeated cycles of unfaithfulness to God, choosing sin, reveling in their sin, and then crying out for God to deliver them from the consequences of their sin.

Rinse, wash, and repeat, and you have the Book of Judges.

Yet still, God chooses them.

Over and over and over.

Fast-forward to the New Testament, and we find Jesus, God made flesh, utilizing the same pattern. To be a disciple of Jesus was to be a disciple of Jesus, together.

God has always had a people.

To follow God has never been to follow God in isolation.

To follow God has always been to follow Him, together.

I recently discussed discipleship with a pastor friend of mine, and he made an astute observation. When we examine Jesus' life, we rarely see Him spending one-on-one time with His disciples. He seemed to disciple in groups.

He called people to salvation individually but discipled them in community.

The 120, the 72, the 50, the 12, the 3.

You know what you don't see in the context of discipleship? The one.

Community is the pattern for following Jesus. When Jesus calls you to follow Him, He not only saves you but adopts you into a family. A family that in many ways has nothing in common but Jesus. Yet in that one thing, we have the most important thing in common.

Sin tried its best to estrange and separate humanity. Yet, through the cross, in the words of Paul,

> *For he himself is our peace, who has made the two groups one and has destroyed the barrier, the dividing wall of hostility, by setting aside in his flesh the law with its commands and regulations. His purpose was to create in himself one new humanity out of the two, thus making peace, and in one body to reconcile both of them to God through the cross, by*

*which he put to death their hostility. He came and preached peace to you who were far away and peace to those who were near. For through him we both have access to the Father by one Spirit. Consequently, you are no longer foreigners and strangers, but fellow citizens with God's people and also members of his household, built on the foundation of the apostles and prophets, with Christ Jesus himself as the chief cornerstone. In him the whole building is joined together and rises to become a holy temple in the Lord. And in him you too are being built together to become a dwelling in which God lives by his Spirit.* (Eph. 2:14-22, NIV)

Ephesians, often referred to as the *Book of the Church*, outlines God's work in forming a people, drawn from every nation, tribe, and language, united in their devotion to Christ and woven together as a single family. God is not building an organization, or a physical, literal building; God is building *a people, a family.*

Part of our identity is belonging to something bigger than us—something ancient, something that begins with God's promise of One to come who will crush the head of the serpent.

Where sin separates us, the blood of Jesus unites us.

Where sin divides based on temporal, cosmetic differences, God declares, "*One new man.*"

Where sin increases strife and envy, the Cross declares, "*One purpose, one mission. His Kingdom come!*"

## Conclusion

Life flows from who you are. And in Christ, our shame is gone—we are not weighed down by who we *used to be*. We have been reunited with our Creator—He knows us fully and invites us to know Him intimately. We have been reunited with other image bearers—we are part of *one* family, established to expand *one* Kingdom that serves *one* King.

The path back to Eden is a path of untold opportunity. I am not who I have been; I am who God has made me. I am known, loved, and accepted by my Creator. I am a part of something bigger than me, and that something is on mission for something eternal.

That is your Christian identity.

Your life flows from there.

Let's recap what we have covered in this book thus far:

- We are born dead in our sin and need to be made alive by the Spirit of God.

- Salvation is spiritual resuscitation.

- At salvation, we are given hope and a mission: to advance God's Kingdom and look forward to the New Heavens and New Earth.

- Not only are we given spiritual life and hope in every situation, but God wants us to flourish in *this life*.

- Flourishing in *this* life flows from our redeemed identity.

After I know who I am, it's time to mature into a dedicated follower of Jesus. Let's break that down in our last few chapters.

chapter 9:
# the first stage of grief

———

*"What we want to know is not, what would this or that man, or this or that Church, have of us, but what Jesus Christ himself wants of us."*

— **Dietrich Bonhoeffer**

I'd guess that when most Christians think about discipleship, a particular passage comes to mind—one where Jesus clearly defines what it means to follow Him. Here it is,

> *Then Jesus said to his disciples, "Whoever wants to be my disciple must deny themselves and take up their cross and follow me. For whoever wants to save their life will lose it, but whoever loses their life for me will find it.* (Matthew 16:24-25, NIV)

Jesus identified three essential ingredients for discipleship: self-denial, cross-bearing, and following. He indicates that true life, *true flourishing,* is on the other side of embracing this formula.

The Bible is full of dichotomies and paradoxes. I would argue the greatest paradox is this: we are dead in sin and need to be brought to life by the Holy Spirit, then to flourish, we need to die.

Die to your flesh.

Die to your sin.

Die to selfishness.

But I am getting ahead of myself.

In this chapter, we will address the first variable of Jesus' formula: the concept of self-denial. What does Jesus mean by '*deny yourself*'? Is He saying to deny what makes me, *me?* Is he saying to embrace a false persona and masquerade as a perfect specimen of humanity?  Do I deny my most innate senses, dreams, hopes, goals, and talents? In short, no.

Yet, Author N.T. Wright says of Jesus,

> *He revealed fully what genuine human life was like—and it turns out to be deeply self-sacrificial. Simply following the desires of the physical body, and equally of the mind, will lead you to ruin.*[68]

Just as Adam illustrates the consequences of rejecting God's command and embracing selfishness, Jesus, the second Adam, exemplifies true humanity and flourishing through His acceptance of His Father's will and surrender of self-interest. But let's walk through what Jesus means.

## Deny What?

The mind is an interesting thing. If you are like me, you can be having a great day.

The birds are chirping.

The sun is out.

*Billy Jean* is turned up to eleven on the drive over to the local hipster coffee shop.

Then, out of nowhere, for no apparent reason, the most morbid, disgusting thought will cross my mind. Why?! What did I do to be slimed by this? Or even worse, is there something deeply wrong with me?

Hopefully, this isn't just me.

---

68    N.T. Wrights, *Paul for Everyone,*(London; Ashford Colour Press, 2002), 19.

What that is is the sin nature rearing its ugly head.

*"Hey! Remember me?!"*

The shrapnel of brokenness we discussed above still plagues our souls. We all have it. Paul addresses this in Romans when he lets us in on his inner dialogue,

> *I do not understand what I do. For what I want to do I do not do, but what I hate I do. And if I do what I do not want to do, I agree that the law is good. As it is, it is no longer I myself who do it, but it is sin living in me. For I know that good itself does not dwell in me, that is, in my sinful nature. For I have the desire to do what is good, but I cannot carry it out. For I do not do the good I want to do, but the evil I do not want to do—this I keep on doing. Now if I do what I do not want to do, it is no longer I who do it, but it is sin living in me that does it.* (Romans 7:15-20, NIV)

Paul is airing his frustrations. He is giving voice to his complaint, *"I want to please God, but then I don't. What is this war within me!?"*

C.S. Lewis astutely observed, *"No man knows how bad he is till he has tried very hard to be good."*[69]

Our soul has two natures at war: the Spirit and the flesh. The regenerated Spirit desires to please God, to submit to His Lordship, and to do all God has commanded. But, in the same body, there is this other nature, this other inkling, this desire to reject God, to give in to what we know is contrary to His will.

---

69  C.S. Lewis, *Mere Christianity* (New York: HarperCollins, 2001), Book III, Chapter 11, 142.

Here's the rub: Giving in to the flesh, the nature opposed to God, feels *great*.

In the moment, nothing is more fun than sin.

Sin offers instant pleasure and delivers.

Sin offers instant satisfaction.

Sin offers happiness.

Sin offers to reward and, in the moment, reward it does.

The problem with sin is not necessarily in the immediate but in its compounding effects. Sin compounded over time equals death.

Spiritual death.

Relational death.

Physical death.

Sin offers microwave results but is a crockpot full o' death.

When Jesus tells his disciples to deny themselves, He is calling for a denial —a rejection of what comes *naturally* to us. We all speak sin fluently; it is our mother tongue. Jesus is calling for a complete rejection of our innate, natural, sinful desires.

I have often heard it said, usually in reference to sexual sin, *"Pastor Jake, I was born this way. So, there is no way it could be wrong. God made me this way."* While I understand the argument and its basis, this argument is not grounded in biblical truth. This argument is based on Rousseau's philosophy, which posits that humans are good by nature and corrupted by society. The biblical perspective teaches that we are naturally flawed, and society is corrupt because the individuals who comprise it are inherently flawed. You are born with various desires that God *did not* hardwire into you; those desires are the result of our sinful nature and the result of the broken, sinful planet that we live on. What feels *natural* to us is often our sinful, corrupted nature. To give into that nature is to reject God's design. Though we are made in the image of God, our sinful nature is also there, corrupting that image. See the previous chapter for more details.

*This* is the reality Jesus is speaking to. Within the human experience is a war of two realities.

Yes, we are made in the image of God.

And yes, we have a sin nature that seeks to draw us away from God's design.

Deny *this*.

Deny the actions that tug at your heartstrings, the desires that run in direct contradiction to the will of God.

## Context of Matthew 16

The most important rule of Biblical interpretation is context. Every verse has a chapter, every chapter has a book, every book has a testament, and each testament has the narrative arc of Scripture. Context is everything. Or as Dan Kimball says, "*Never read a bible verse*".[70] Meaning, don't pluck a verse out of its context. That's a good way to start a cult. And I'm sure none of you want to be the next David Koresh.

70    Dan Kimball, *How (NOT) to Read the Bible,*(Grand Rapids, MI: Zondervan, 2020), 39.

In Matthew 16, Jesus asked the disciples who the people thought He was. The disciples quickly name the who's who of Second Temple Judaism: John the Baptist, Elijah, Jeremiah, or one of the other prophets. Then, Jesus makes it personal and asks who *they* think He is. Peter is the first one to answer, "*You are the Messiah, the Son of the living God.*" (Matthew 16:16, NIV) Jesus let it be known that this answer was a download directly from heaven, and upon this revelation, Jesus would build His people, His community, His Church.

The text then pivots as Jesus teaches His disciples about how and why He must suffer from that time forward. Peter, the same Peter who just had a direct revelation from heaven, begins to rebuke Jesus.

To be clear, Peter rebukes God.

He rebukes the idea of suffering, of the cross, of persecution by the religious elite.

To this, Jesus says, "*Get behind me, Satan. You are a stumbling block to me; you do not have in mind the concerns of God, but merely human concerns.*" (Matt. 16:23, NIV)

Peter goes from receiving a divine revelation—recognizing Jesus for who He truly is—to being rebuked as Satan *by Jesus* for opposing God's mission and urging Jesus to avoid the path of suffering. It is in this context that Jesus says, "*Whoever wants to be my disciple must deny themselves and take up their cross and follow me.*" (Matt. 16:24, NIV)

Jesus seems to be laying out this truth:

> *True discipleship requires a denial of the self—self-motivation, self-preservation, self-exaltation—and a dedication to see God's will be done regardless of the cost.*

The first step in this process is an *intentional* denial, a rejection of the tug to elevate the desires of sin over the desire to please God.

## Paul and Walking New

Paul wrote to local churches, addressing issues specific to each church. Much like today, the local churches were filled with people from diverse backgrounds and life experiences before they came to know Christ. As a result, a large part of Paul's letters focused on guiding believers on how to live out their new identity. In most of his letters, Paul has a "how-to-follow-Jesus" three-part formula. His three-part formula directly corresponds with Jesus' three-part definition of discipleship.

| Jesus | Paul |
|---|---|
| Deny yourself | Put off your old self |
| Pick up your cross | Be crucified to the world |
| Follow Me | Put on new self |

**"**

*"True discipleship requires a denial of the self—self-motivation, self-preservation, self-exaltation—and a dedication to see God's will be done regardless of the cost."*

**"**

Paul makes it clear that there is a distinct way believers in Jesus are called to live. He writes to the Ephesians,

> *So I tell you this, and insist on it in the Lord, that you must no longer live as the Gentiles do, in the futility of their thinking They are darkened in their understanding and separated from the life of God because of the ignorance that is in them due to the hardening of their hearts' Having lost all sensitivity, they have given themselves over to sensuality so as to indulge in every kind of impurity, and they are full of greed.* (Eph. 4:17-19, NIV)

Prior to the outpouring of the Holy Spirit, the Gentile world was largely excluded from the people of God. Natural, ethnic Israel were the people of God. They had the Torah, the commandments, and the practice of circumcision. They were on the inside; the Gentile world was on the outside. As outsiders, they acted like outsiders. They did not have the Law and acted like it.

So, rather than obeying God through general revelation[71], that is, conscience and nature, they indulged in every bodily urge. Paul's point is simple: you were once Gentiles on the

---

71   In theology, the Doctrine of Revelation essentially asserts that God is a speaking God who has revealed who He is to mankind. Within the Doctrine of Revelation are two main types of revelation: General Revelation and Special Revelation. General Revelation is revelation given to all humanity proving that God exists. General Revelation is primary experienced through creation, conscience and common grace. Special Revelation is specific revelation to specific people at specific times. For more details see, Kevin J.Conner, Ken Malmin, *The Foundations of Christian Doctrine*, Portland, OR; City Christian Publishing, 1982. Or Mark Driscoll, Gary Breshears, *Doctrine*, Wheaton, IL.: Crossway, 2019.

outside looking in, *but now*, you have been grafted in, *you are* the people of God, so deny what you used to do and instead live according to your new identity. He continues,

> *That, however, is not the way of life you learned when you heard about Christ and were taught in him in accordance with the truth that is in Jesus. You were taught, with regard to your former way of life, to put off your old self, which is being corrupted by its deceitful desires.* (Eph. 4:20-22, NIV)

Once we have encountered the risen Savior, there is a new standard, a new way to live. We deny, we reject the way we *used to live*, we pursue the upward call in Christ Jesus.

We once lived in sexual promiscuity, but now we reject that way of life and embrace a biblical view of sexuality. We once lived in greed and materialism, but now we turn from that and embrace biblical generosity. We used to allow culture to define our values. Now, we reject that and allow the Word of God to define our values. We used to be driven by emotions. Now, though we give voice to our emotions, we are led by the Spirit. We once prioritized self-satisfaction above all else, but now we reject that pursuit and commit ourselves to building what God is building— namely, His Church.

The Old Testament is full of the language of "*stop doing evil, learn the good, and then do that good.*" The prophet Isaiah begins to prophesy during the reign of Uzziah. He prophesied to both Israel and Judah, calling them to *return* to God. Remember that the most frequent word used to depict the idea of *repentance* in the Old Testament is *return.*

Return to the law.

Return to obedience to the law.

Return to God.

In the opening chapter of Isaiah, God is ticked. He is sick of religious ritual without repentance. He is sick of empty sacrifices, holy days, and festivals; He wants the hearts of His people. God says through Isaiah, midway through chapter 1,

> *Wash yourselves; make yourselves clean;*
> *remove the evil of your deeds from before my eyes;*
> *cease to do evil,*
> *learn to do good;*
> *seek justice,*
> *correct oppression;*
> *bring justice to the fatherless,*
> *plead the widow's cause.* (Isaiah 1:16-17, ESV)

What is God saying? *Stop* living a sinful life, *learn* to do what I have called you to, and then *do it*. This is the threefold command of Jesus, echoed in Paul, and found throughout Scripture.

Going back to Matthew 16, following Peter's rejection of Jesus' teaching on the Cross, Jesus calls His disciples to no longer let their sinful, fallen nature dictate their actions. But to first deny themselves. Deny their selfish urges, their knee-jerk reaction for instant gratification. Paul says it this way,

> *For if you live according to the flesh, you will die; but if by the Spirit you put to death the misdeeds of the body, you will live.* (Romans 8:13, NIV)

True flourishing begins by living in alignment with your new identity in Christ. If I am the righteousness of God, if I have been transferred to the Kingdom of light, if I am a son of the King, if I am in the family of God, then I have new responsibilities. I am not who I used to be, so I need to stop doing what I used to do.

Deny yourself.

Put to death the deeds of the flesh.

Don't live like the Gentiles.

Put off your old self.

Live like a follower of Jesus.

In the words of G.K. Chesterton, *"A dead thing can go with the stream, but only a living thing can go against it."*[72]

---

72   G.K. Chesterton, The Everlasting Man, (San Francisco: Ignatius Press, 1993), 208.

chapter 10:

# Jesus and a side of french fries

---

*"Just as Christ is Christ only in virtue of his suffering and rejection, so the disciple is a disciple only in so far as he shares his Lord's suffering and rejection and crucifixion. Discipleship means adherence to the person of Jesus, and therefore submission to the law of Christ is the law of the cross."*

**— Dietrich Bonhoeffer**

I have never been a fan of Halloween. This likely comes from my parents, who taught me about the realities of spiritual warfare from an early age. Now, don't get me wrong; I love dressing my kids up cute and loading them up with candy so I can exact what they have deemed the "Daddy tax."

My kids knock on doors to get free candy for *me*? Score.

But the creepy stuff is a no-go. The demonic, the horror elements have never been attractive. It brings back horrible memories of the guy who lived next door when I was growing up. This guy loved Halloween. And not the cute, fun, playful side. He loved the horror; he reveled in inducing nightmares. Year after year, his front yard was full of demented imagery. One year, he had a guillotine that came hurling to the earth, separating a head from its body, and below it lay a basket full of severed heads. Another year, he adorned his front window with an electric chair and enhanced the strobe light-filled display with the sound of a screaming man that reverberated through the suburban neighborhood.

I guess he had a thing for torture devices.

When you take time to read through history, it becomes clear that humans are sick in the head. Humans have an insatiable lust for more, stopping at nothing to obtain it. The fifteenth through seventeenth centuries were marked by wars over control of the spice trade.

Think about that.

People died for spices.

The greed of man knows no limit. They will rape, pillage, kill, torture, and harm whoever stands in their way. Every civilization is guilty; it seems one of the greatest common denominators amongst humanity throughout time and space is their capacity to inflict pain.

Aleksandr Solzhenitsyn, a Russian historian and novelist, wrote his masterpiece, *The Gulag Archipelago,* after serving eight years in a Soviet gulag for criticizing Stalin. This incredible work is divided into multiple volumes and examines the juxtaposition between human beauty and their capacity for brutality. Solzhenitsyn soberly notes, *"The line dividing good and evil cuts through the heart of every human being."*[73]

I've recently been shaken by how familiar we have become with one specific ancient torture device.

It has become a tattoo, a fashion piece, a necklace.

That torture device is none other than the cross.

In Western society, constant exposure to the cross has dulled our sense of its profound meaning. What, at one time, caused horror has become white noise.

It's hard to track who invented crucifixion; many cultures have used some form of hanging from the extremities as a form of execution. One commentator includes *"the Assyrians, the people of India, the Scythians, the Taurians, the Thracians, the Celts, the Germans, the Britons, the Numidians, and the*

---

73    Aleksandr Solzhenitsyn, *The Gulag Archipelago, 1918–1956: An Experiment in Literary Investigation,* trans. Thomas P. Whitney (New York: Harper & Row, 1974), Part I, Chapter 4, 168.

*Carthaginians*"[74] when listing cultures that engaged in some form of crucifixion.

But the Roman invention of the cross was particularly brutal.

Many historians believe the Romans "borrowed" crucifixion from the Carthaginians. And even the Romans thought crucifixion too "barbaric" for their own citizens, so they reserved it for slaves and aliens.[75]

The cross of the Romans took three forms,

1. A vertical stake with no crossbeam.

2. A vertical stake with a crossbeam, shaped like a capital T.

3. A vertical stake with an intersecting beam— the shape traditionally celebrated in Christian iconography.[76]

Before crucifixion, several events would take place. First, the victim was often tortured with rods or whips. This torture could even include amputating certain body parts. Next, if the victim was to be crucified on a cross with a crossbeam, the victim was forced to carry his *patibulum,* the crossbeam of the cross. Then, he was attached with either nails or ropes and lifted up to the already fixed beam or tree for execution.

---

74    David A. Fiensy, "Crucifixion," ed. John D. Barry et al., *The Lexham Bible Dictionary* (Bellingham, WA: Lexham Press, 2016).

75    Walter A. Elwell and Barry J. Beitzel, "Crucifixion," *Baker Encyclopedia of the Bible* (Grand Rapids, MI: Baker Book House, 1988), 555.

76    Fiensy, "Crucifixion," ed. John D. Barry et al., *The Lexham Bible Dictionary.*

Finally, the agonizing wait ensued; death could take days. Writing in the third century, Pseudo-Manetho writes,

> Punished on their tortured [bodies], they see the stake (i.e., cross) as their fate. In the bitterest of torment, they have been fastened with nails, [to become] evil banquets for birds and terrible scraps for dogs.[77]

Seneca describes a similar scene in the first century, saying,

> Can anyone be found who would prefer wasting away in pain, dying limb by limb, or letting out his life drop by drop, rather than expiring once for all? Can any man be found willing to be fastened to the accursed tree, long sickly, already deformed, swelling with ugly tumours on chest and shoulders, and draw the breath of life amid long—drawn-out agony?[78]

When we envision crosses, grand and elevated altars often come to mind; yet, historically, they were scarcely taller than the person nailed to them. The tormentors designed them low enough to allow animals to gnaw on the body post-mortem.

The Romans crucified criminals in public places as a warning to all, "*This is the fate of those who cross the empire.*" Those crucified were naked, bloodied, and beaten. They eventually died by bleeding out or suffocation as their lungs filled with blood. Crucifixion was a horrible spectacle, meant to drive fear into all who witnessed.

So, when Jesus tells His disciples to "*pick you your cross,*" imagine the thoughts the disciples must have had. Keep in

---

77   Fiensy, "Crucifixion," ed. John D. Barry et al., *The Lexham Bible Dictionary*.

78   Fiensy, "Crucifixion," ed. John D. Barry et al., *The Lexham Bible Dictionary*.

mind that this is *before* Jesus was crucified. When we think of the cross, we think of Jesus; when they thought of the cross, they thought of the penalty imposed on the worst among them by an oppressive force.

Crucifixion meant death.

*"Is Jesus saying that to be a disciple, I need to die?"*

Simply put, yes, that is what He is saying.

## Paul and Crucifixion

The concept of the cross is everywhere in the New Testament. Philippians, one of Paul's letters from prison, is a great example.

At the end of the book, Paul, like a Pentecostal preacher, starts his "soft close" to the letter and encourages the church to rejoice in the Lord. He then goes on to give them reasons to rejoice, and it has nothing to do with natural accomplishments. After describing his impressive resume, he says,

> But whatever gain I had, I counted as loss for the sake of Christ. Indeed, I count everything as loss because of the surpassing worth of knowing Christ Jesus my Lord. For his sake I have suffered the loss of all things and count them as rubbish, in order that I may gain Christ and be found in him, not having a righteousness of my own that comes from the law, but that which comes through faith in Christ, the righteousness from God that depends on faith— that I may know him and the power of his resurrection, and may share his sufferings, becoming like him in his death, that by any means possible I may attain the resurrection from the dead. (Phil. 3:8-11, ESV)

Paul has a simple point: in comparison to Jesus, nothing else comes close. He is the aim, the prize, the goal; all else is *loss* in comparison to the splendor of Jesus.

Then, it takes a dark twist.

Paul says he wants to share Christ's sufferings and become like Him in death.

Wait, what?

Suffer.

Die.

That seems off.

However, this is a *major* doctrine in the New Testament.

Again, the Bible is full of paradoxes and dichotomies. Once more, let me sum up all that we have covered in this book with one confusing but accurate sentence:

> *We are spiritually dead and need to be made alive. Then, we need to die to truly live.*

The process of following Jesus is strange. We begin by realizing our poverty of spirit. We are dead and need the Holy Spirit to resuscitate us, to breathe life into us just as He breathed life into Adam's nostrils. But after we have been brought to life, to live according to design requires an intentional, deliberate act of us dying, daily, moment by moment, thought by thought, sometimes breath by breath.

**"**

*"We are spiritually dead and need to be made alive. Then, we need to die to truly live."*

**"**

You are dead and need to be brought to life so you can die and truly live.

Earlier, I mentioned the pattern we find in Pauline literature and how it aligns with Jesus' command to deny yourself, pick up your cross, and follow.

**Step 1**: Jesus said deny yourself; Paul phrased it as 'Put off your old self.'

**Step 2:** Jesus said, 'Pick up your cross.' Paul says, 'You are crucified to the world and to your sin.'

**Step 3:** Jesus says, "Follow me." Paul writes, "…put on the new self…"

We begin the journey toward true human flourishing by denying and turning away from our broken, sinful nature. But turning from sin is not enough. We must kill it. Paul writes about this to just about every church he can. Here are some potent examples,

> *I have been crucified with Christ. It is no longer I who live, but Christ who lives in me. And the life I now live in the flesh I live by faith in the Son of God, who loved me and gave himself for me.* (Galatians 2:20, ESV)

> *And those who belong to Christ Jesus have crucified the flesh with its passions and desires.* (Galatians 5:24, ESV)

> *Put to death therefore what is earthly in you: sexual immorality, impurity, passion, evil desire, and covetousness, which is idolatry.* (Colossians 3:5, ESV)

> *For if you live according to the flesh you will die, but if by the*
> *Spirit you put to death the deeds of the body, you will live.*
> (Romans 8:13, ESV)

Paul repeatedly stresses the importance of the disciple of Jesus identifying with Jesus and His crucifixion. Just as Jesus was crucified for the sins of the world, so we must crucify our sinful nature, let it die, and live according to the design God has for us.

## Burger King

I love Burger King. I love their double cheeseburgers. I love their fries. I love the flame-grilled Whopper. I love the little apple pie things you can get. I love the assorted Oreo desserts. I love the choices, the options; at Burger King, you can have it your way. As one of their recent ads states, *"Why eat with a clown when you can dine with a king."*

I imagine many of you are like me and love to be able to customize and sort through a plethora of options until something strikes your fancy. The joys of picking and choosing, rejecting what seems inferior. As the kids would say, these are first-world problems.

Unfortunately, these first-world problems have leaked into Western Christianity. We want our perfectly manicured lives, with our meticulously structured five-year and ten-year plans, with a little sprinkle of Jesus on top. We take our Rolodex of life options to Jesus and ask Him to bless what we already have going on.

*"Jesus, I have already done all the legwork. I just need a little divine favor to be poured out on my elbow grease."*

There is one minor problem, *that* looks nothing like biblical, Jesus-centered Christianity. Biblical, Jesus-centered Christianity clears the table of all other agendas, desires, hopes, dreams, and cries out like Jesus did in Gethsemane, *"Nevertheless, not my will, but yours, be done."* (Luke 22:42, ESV)

*That* is the crucified life.

*That* is carrying your cross.

To wake up each day and say, *"God, whatever You will today"* is to live crucified. To approach Jesus as Lord by submitting to His definition of sexuality, and generosity, and marriage, and politics.

To not only deny our sinful desires but to lay them down before Jesus, crucifying them, and learning the ways of the Spirit.

The crucified life is submitted to the designs and definitions of God.

Carrying your cross looks like living like Jesus.

Yet, all of that is easier said than done. The ways of Jesus are *simple* but not *easy.* The longer I follow Jesus, the more frustrated I become with how pesky sin is. How do I still struggle with some of the same messed-up patterns I did a decade ago? Maybe you are like me. You feel like you are doing great in your walk with Jesus, and then, BAM! There sin is, crouching at the door.

Sin is like cockroaches; apparently, they both survive nuclear winters.

To live crucified is to willingly submit to God's plan for every aspect of our lives and endeavor to kill the sin that lurks within us.

## The Cross and the Public

Denying yourself, picking up your cross, all of this plays out in front of people. It can be embarrassing. Crucifixion was public, and it took a long time to accomplish its goal. History shows us,

> In *the Roman Empire, a convicted criminal, when taken to be crucified, was forced to carry his own cross. This showed publicly that he was then under and submissive to the rule he had been opposing. Likewise, Jesus' disciples must demonstrate their submission to the One against whom they had rebelled.*[79]

Consider this: just as the condemned carried their cross showing the crowds they were *unwillingly* submitted to the Roman authority, so as Christ followers, we *willingly* carry our cross, demonstrating to the world that in all things, we submit to Christ.

The crucified life is both intensely personal and horrifically public. Personally, killing the sinful nature takes a long time.

---

79    Louis A. Barbieri Jr., "Matthew," in *The Bible Knowledge Commentary: An Exposition of the Scriptures*, ed. J. F. Walvoord and R. B. Zuck, vol. 2 (Wheaton, IL: Victor Books, 1985), 59.

Yet, the idea of crucifying our sin identifies us with our Lord's sufferings, but it is also a great reminder of the marathon we are in as disciples. Looking like Jesus takes time—decades, a lifetime. And even still, it's imperfect.

I have learned that God loves the process and loves to take His time.

He is not a microwave God; He is a crockpot God.

He uses decades and lifetimes to refine His people.

Noah was 600 years old at the Flood. Abraham was 100 years old when Isaac was born. Moses was 80 years old at the Burning Bush. David had to wait 15-20 years between his anointing to be king and ascending to the throne, and the wait was filled with running, fear, and pain. Even Paul had to wait 12-14 years between his conversion and his first missionary journey.

God uses time as a tool to refine His chosen vessels.

And crucifying the flesh, the sinful nature takes time.

The crucified life also plays out publicly; the world watches as we become more like Christ. As we strive to be like Jesus, failing along the way, spectators abound, but our aim should be to mimic the condemned in the first century, carrying our crossbeam, willingly submitted to Jesus' way, through His life, according to His truth.

## Reeducation

In closing this chapter, I also want to mention one other aspect of living the crucified life: reeducation. To take up the cross means to unlearn and relearn. We must unlearn the ways of the world and learn the ways of the Kingdom.

In the Bible, the word *"world"* is used in several ways. The first refers to the planet and its inhabitants. The world is the place we live; it's our neighbors, our schools, and our society. When this concept of the *world* is used, the Bible is clear that God loves the world, and so should we. However, the second use of the *world* refers to the systems and ways of our sinful reality.

John writes about this when he says,

> *Do not love the world or the things in the world. If anyone loves the world, the love of the Father is not in him. For all that is in the world—the desires of the flesh and the desires of the eyes and pride of life—is not from the Father but is from the world. And the world is passing away along with its desires, but whoever does the will of God abides forever.* (1 John 2:15-17, ESV)

John refers to the broken planet we inhabit and the sinful *ways* of the world; to live for Jesus, to live the crucified life, is to reject the ways of the world and embrace the ways of Jesus. To take the *ancient path* to life, hope, and flourishing.

Over the past two centuries or so, the West has experienced a unique period in church history where, oddly enough, the values of the pervading society corresponded, to a degree, with the values of the Christian faith. Christianity was trendy.

However, that era has come to an end, and our era is increasingly reflecting the social dynamics that characterized much of early Christianity. Ages when true Christianity and its values ran in direct opposition to the values of the pervading culture.

Christians must choose between the values of the world and the values of Jesus.

To live crucified is to choose in every waking moment that Jesus is better.

His way is better.

His Word is better.

His design is better.

Living the crucified life means purposely denying sinful cravings and striving, endeavoring to reflect the goodness of Jesus. When spectators see our crucified life, they should smell the aroma of Jesus. This leads us to our final chapter, which discusses Jesus' invitation to "Follow me."

chapter 11:
# who's in charge here?

---

*"Christ calls, the disciple follows: that is grace and commandment in one."*
— **Dietrich Bonhoeffer**

I'm the firstborn of four. The alpha male and heir to the birthright. The brightest and best-looking. Here's hoping all three of my siblings read this so they are reminded of their depraved, second-rate status in the Taylor lineage.

In all seriousness, being the firstborn is strange. From the moment that second kid sucks air, you are ordained leader of the kids. Somehow, responsibility slides onto your plate. You should "know better" at five. I was the Lord of the Flies.

I find the very concept of leadership odd; some humans have sway over others, and some are looking to be swayed. As John Maxwell says, *"Leadership is influence, nothing more, nothing less."*[80] The problem with leadership being influence is that influence can be heard and ignored. Influence is just that, influence. It's nothing binding; it has little more power than suggestion.

When considering Jesus, many Christians simply see Jesus as their leader. Jesus *influences* my life, my decisions, my choices.

Yet, Jesus' call to discipleship is not Him saying, *"I want to influence the way you live your life."*

No, He is saying, 'I *want* your life.'

The whole of it.

*Jesus is not interested in compartmentalized discipleship.*

Jesus' invitation to *"follow me"* is an invitation to burn the ships, put all your eggs in His basket, cross the Rubicon.

---

80    John C. Maxwell, *The 21 Irrefutable Laws of Leadership: Follow Them and People Will Follow You* (Nashville: Thomas Nelson, 2007), 17.

Pick your figure of speech.

When Jesus says, *"deny yourself, pick up your cross, and follow me,"* He means to follow Him with reckless abandon.

This reminds me of how I clean my house. My wife and I are very different people. We are both strong personalities; we are what some might dare to call stubborn. One of our most significant differences is the way we value a clean space. I am a bit of a neat freak; I believe everything in my home has a home, and if an item is not in its home, then that item must be homesick. My duty is to return said item to its home the moment it leaves.

My wife, four-year-old, and six-year-old don't seem to agree.

Often, when we have people coming over, we do a speed clean; everyone runs through the house, grabbing all the laundry, toys, and random paraphernalia as we go. Then, we stuff it into some unsuspecting room or closet. We have a clear strategy; our guests are free to roam about the kitchen, living room, and bathroom, but the mess-infested room or closet is off-limits. They have access to our carefully manicured spaces, but the spaces that house the *real* mess are inaccessible.

Many Christians approach following Jesus in the same manner; there are areas of life where Jesus is allowed access, and other areas that are off-limits. Jesus is welcome to bless us, heal us, prosper us, and give us those Holy Ghost goose bumps. But by no means are we open to correction, discipline, or conviction.

However, Jesus' call is an invitation to tear down every barrier, bring our mess into the light, and acknowledge our brokenness. It's a call to total surrender and the vulnerability that comes with it.

We can only go one direction at a time; we either follow Jesus wholeheartedly or we do not.

## Old Testament Walking

Following Jesus requires motion and movement.

To follow Jesus, one must walk after Him.

Throughout Scripture, "walking" is used as a metaphor for how one lives life.

For example, a few months ago, I was reading through 2 Chronicles, and a trend began to grab my attention. When describing the kings, the writer described them as walking like one of two characters: David or Jeroboam.

David is an interesting case study. Scripture calls him the *"Man After God's Own Heart."*[81] Yet, when you look at the life of David, he leaves a lot to be desired.

When David was on the run from Saul, the Bible records that scores of eclectic characters began to follow him,

> *David departed from there and escaped to the cave of Adullam. And when his brothers and all his father's house heard it, they went down there to him. And everyone who was in distress, and everyone who was in debt, and everyone*

---

> *who was bitter in soul, gathered to him. And he became*
> *commander over them. And there were with him about four*
> *hundred men.* (1 Samuel 22:1-2 ESV)

Scores of those in distress, in debt, and embittered surround David. Talk about a rough crowd. Yet, out of this bunch, eventually, comes a group known as David's Mighty Men. They accomplished incredible feats of strength and valor, following David through hell and high water. They fled for their lives when David was afraid for his. Because David was being pursued by a mad king, so were they.

Numbered among them was a man named Uriah the Hittite. Uriah was by David's side before his ascension to the throne, demonstrating loyalty and friendship. And apparently, Uriah's wife was quite the looker.

One day, King David, now fully experiencing kingship as foretold by the prophet Samuel, sent his army to war while he enjoyed the luxury of the palace. He decided to stroll up to the rooftop, where he saw the wife of Uriah, the wife of one of his mighty men, the wife of a man who had been by his side through fear, danger, obscurity, and now royalty. And she is bathing. He decides she is pleasing to the eye, calls for her, sleeps with her, and gets her pregnant. He then tries to cover up his sin, but Uriah is too honorable to sleep with Bathsheba while his brothers in arms are at war. So, David arranges to have him killed. David, *"Man After God's Own Heart"*, commits adultery with a loyal friend's wife, and then kills him to cover up his sin.

Not only is he an adulterer and murderer, but by all accounts, he is a terrible father. One specific example involves his son Absalom. Absalom had a half-brother named Amnon who fell in love with his half-sister, and Absalom's full-blood sister, Tamar. Amnon's "love" led to rape, which enraged Absalom and ultimately led to Amnon's murder.

David was heartbroken over the conflict that was tearing his family apart and grieved for Amnon. After three years in exile, Absalom was allowed to return, yet David still refused to see him for another two years. David explicitly says in 2 Samuel, "*Let him dwell apart in his own house; he is not to come into my presence.*" So, Absalom lived apart in his own house and did not come into the king's presence." (2 Sam. 14:24, ESV) So, Amnon was murdered, and David refused to see his son Absalom for five full years. Two of those years, they were neighbors in the same city.

I say this to say that David being called the *"Man After God's Own Heart"* in the eternal canon of Scripture, from a human perspective, is weird. So, there must have been something else in David's life that showed what it means to pursue God's heart.

We find that answer when we combine Psalm 51 and 2 Samuel 12. God sends Nathan the prophet to confront David about his sin with Bathsheba, and his response is recorded in holy writ.

> *Have mercy on me, O God,*
> *according to your steadfast love;*
> *according to your abundant mercy*

*blot out my transgressions.*
*Wash me thoroughly from my iniquity,*
*and cleanse me from my sin!*

*For I know my transgressions,*
*and my sin is ever before me.*
*Against you, you only, have I sinned*
*and done what is evil in your sight,*
*so that you may be justified* in your words
*and blameless in your judgment.* (Psalm 51:1-4, ESV)

David is called the *"Man After God's Own Heart"* not because of an illusion of perfection but because of an attitude of repentance. To walk in the way of David is to walk in repentance. David, though broken and sinful, responded quickly to conviction and pursued the heart of God.

He *walked* after God.

He *followed* Him.

The life of a disciple is consumed with a desire to be more like God. Disciples desire, above all else, to better reflect the image of God. The disciple of Jesus has a heart that cries what David does in Psalm 139, *"Search me, O God, and know my heart! Try me and know my thoughts! And see if there be any grievous way in me and **lead me in the way everlasting**!"* (Psalm 139: 23-24, ESV)

That is walking in the way of David.

Not a walk of perfection but a walk of repentance.

A life lived, a walk walked in pursuit of God.

A life that echoes the heart of Paul when he writes,

> *Indeed, I count everything as loss because of the surpassing worth of knowing Christ Jesus my Lord. For his sake I have suffered the loss of all things and count them as rubbish, in order that I may gain Christ.* (Philippians 3:8, ESV)

Juxtapose that with those who are described as walking in the manner of Jeroboam. Jeroboam was introduced in 1 Kings and was the first king of the Northern tribes of Israel. Fearing a split devotion due to the temple's location in Judah, Jeroboam constructs two golden calves—one in Dan and one in Bethel—reminiscent of the Golden Calf described in the Book of Exodus. He implores his people to worship these calves rather than travel to the temple. Thus, the legacy of Jeroboam is one of idolatry, that is, worshipping something other than the true God. To walk in the way of Jeroboam is to refuse to follow the ways of God and shun the fear of the Lord.

John Calvin famously wrote, "*The human mind is, so to speak, a perpetual forge of idols.*"[82] Idolatry is allowing anything other than God to steal affection. When anything else takes preeminence in our heart, in our minds, in our emotions, we have succumbed to idolatry. Pastor and Theologian Tim Keller described the Bible's teaching on idolatry: "*The Bible uses three basic metaphors to describe how people relate to the idols of their hearts. They love idols, trust idols, and obey idols.*"[83]

---

82    Elliot Ritzema, 300 Quotations for Preachers from the Reformation, Pastorum Series (Bellingham, WA: Lexham Press, 2013).

83    Timothy Keller, *Counterfeit Gods: The Empty Promises of Money, Sex, and Power, and the Only Hope That Matters* (New York: Dutton, 2009)xxi.

Loving, trusting, and obeying is *exactly* how we are designed to interact with God.

Not a single king over the northern tribes—referred to as Israel in Kings and Chronicles—followed the ways of David or acted righteously. As a result, the Assyrians eventually conquered them and took them into exile, leading to what is now known as the "*Ten Lost Tribes of Israel.*" Descendants from this lineage ultimately became Samaritans in the first century.

So, two ways of walking: the way of David or the way of Jeroboam.

Walking in repentance and fidelity to God or walking in idolatry.

There is no third option.

The metaphor of walking to describe our relationship with God didn't originate with the kings—it began with Abraham, "*The Father of the Faith.*" God tells Abraham, "*I am God Almighty; walk before me, and be blameless...*" (Genesis 17:1, ESV) This reference marks the beginning of a deeply rooted understanding within the Jewish community that to walk before God is to obey and submit to God. Again, walking is a metaphor for the way we live life.

## The New Testament and Walking

The concept of walking in the way of God or the way of the world, or Baal, or Jeroboam, is everywhere in the New Testament. One of our earliest church guides, *The Didache* (The Teaching) from the late first century, believed to be a practical manual for church life, opens with, "*There are two ways, one of life and one of death; but there is a great difference between them.*"[84]

The *Didache* then expands on the "*way of life*" by urging obedience to Jesus' teachings as outlined in the Sermon on the Mount.

Jesus' invitation to "*follow me*" wasn't a revolutionary concept; He was pleading with those in His hearing to return to an ancient path, the true path, to walk in the way of David.

Jesus saw Himself as the fulfillment of all the Old Testament; He was the culmination of every prophecy, every story, every psalm, and proverb. He is the climax.

When Jesus shows up, the God of the universe shows up. The same God who spoke to Abraham and told him, "*Walk before me, and be blameless*", is the God who calls His disciples to the same decision, but now with a new revelation.

Before Jesus goes to the cross, Jesus plainly tells the Twelve, "*I am the way, and the truth, and the life. No one comes to the Father except through me.*" (John 14:6, ESV)

Think about this concept.

He is the way: the path we walk on.

The truth: the way we walk.

The life: the goal at the end of the path.

Deny yourselves.

---

84  The Didache: The Teaching of the Twelve Apostles, ed. Douglas J. Michalak (Las Vegas, 2021), 4.

Pick up your cross.

Follow me.

To follow Jesus is to cease to follow all other voices.

I follow; He leads.

## Following 101

Too often, theological concepts seem theoretical. How do some of these concepts play out practically? How do I follow someone who is not physically on the planet? So glad you asked. I want to answer this question in two main ways:

1.  Through the person of the Holy Spirit

When Jesus called the Twelve to follow Him, He called them to literally, physically follow Him. That is why the Gospels record the disciples leaving their nets, or their tax booths, leaving all behind, to cling to Jesus.

Obviously, we cannot physically follow the incarnate Son of God today. So, what does following Jesus look like in the 21$^{st}$ century? Before Calvary, Jesus had the Passover meal with His disciples. John provides the most detailed account of the conversation at the table, covering a myriad of topics— essentially serving as Jesus' farewell address, apart from His post-resurrection teachings.

One major topic is especially pertinent to our conversation; He discusses the role of the third person of the Trinity, the Holy Spirit. Jesus makes a few shocking claims about this person,

**"**

"He is the way: the path we walk on.
The truth: the way we walk.
The life: the goal at the end of the path."

**"**

*And I will ask the Father, and he will give you another Helper, to be with you forever, even the Spirit of truth, whom the world cannot receive, because it neither sees him nor knows him. You know him, for he dwells with you and will be in you. But the Helper, the Holy Spirit, whom the Father will send in my name, he will teach you all things and bring to your remembrance all that I have said to you.* (John 14:16-17, ESV)

*But now I am going to him who sent me, and none of you asks me, 'Where are you going?' But because I have said these things to you, sorrow has filled your heart. Nevertheless, I tell you the truth: it is to your advantage that I go away, for if I do not go away, the Helper will not come to you. But if I go, I will send him to you. And when he comes, he will convict the world concerning sin and righteousness and judgment...When the Spirit of truth comes, he will guide you into all the truth, for he will not speak on his own authority, but whatever he hears he will speak, and he will declare to you the things that are to come. He will glorify me, for he will take what is mine and declare it to you. All that the Father has is mine; therefore I said that he will take what is mine and declare it to you.* (John 16:5-8, 13-15, ESV)

First, Jesus makes one thing abundantly clear: He is leaving. He is about to finish His mission, and then He is out; Jesus didn't pull an Irish Goodbye. I am an extroverted introvert, a practitioner of Irish Goodbyes for decades.

Alas, I digress.

Imagine being the disciples; they walked with Jesus for three years. They saw blind eyes opened, deaf ears unstopped, the dead walk out of tombs. And now, it's just over? He is *leaving?*

Not only is He leaving, but Jesus had the audacity to say that His leaving was a good thing, to *their* advantage. How could that possibly be?

One of the first doctrines any seminary student studies is the Doctrine of God, which addresses the age-old question: *Who is God?* Part of that doctrine involves studying the communicable and incommunicable attributes of God. The *communicable attributes* are those that humanity can demonstrate due to the *imago Dei*, albeit imperfectly. For example, God *is* love, so as image bearers we have the capacity to love. God *is* truth; we have both the capacity for and desire for truth. God *is* good, so we have a longing and capacity for goodness.

However, God also has *incommunicable attributes*; these are attributes that belong to God and God alone. Some of those attributes are the omnis: omnipresence, omnipotence, and omniscience. This means that God is everywhere all the time, all-powerful, and all-knowing.

When we talk about God putting on skin and bones, the Word being made flesh, one truth we wrestle with is how Jesus willingly and temporarily laid down some of those omnis. Paul hints at this when he writes,

> *Have this mind among yourselves, which is yours in Christ Jesus, who, though he was in the form of God, did not count*

*equality with God a thing to be grasped, but emptied himself,*
*by taking the form of a servant, being born in the likeness of*
*men.* (Philippians 2:5-7, ESV)

Robert P. Lightner comments on this passage, "*As God, He*
*had all the rights of deity, and yet during His incarnate state He*
*surrendered His right to manifest Himself visibly as the God of all*
*splendor and glory.*"[85]

One of those omni's that Jesus willingly *emptied* Himself of,
for a time, was omnipresence. When Jesus was physically
walking on the planet, He was in one place at one time. If
Jesus was in Galilee, He was not in Jerusalem. Jesus put on
confinement and limitation to fulfill His salvific purpose.
After the Cross and His subsequent resurrection, Jesus makes
it abundantly clear that salvation would be extended to
everyone everywhere.

That is a big mission.

A mission so big it would take the omnis.

Which is where the Holy Spirit steps in.

It was better for Jesus to go because a cosmic tag-team was
taking place. Jesus, having accomplished the plan of salvation,
was passing the proverbial baton to the person of the Holy
Spirit to continue Jesus' ministry in and through the Church.
Now, through the Spirit of Jesus, the Holy Spirit, every
believer can have the advantage of the presence of God.

---

85    Robert P. Lightner, "Philippians," in *The Bible Knowledge Commentary:*
      *An Exposition of the Scriptures*, ed. J. F. Walvoord and R. B. Zuck, vol. 2
      (Wheaton, IL: Victor Books, 1985), 654.

In Jesus' discourse on the Holy Spirit in the Gospel of John, He emphasizes three key roles the Spirit will play:

A.    The Holy Spirit Indwells Believers

Jesus lays out that the person of the Holy Spirit will take up residence *in* believers forever. Wherever you go, the Holy Spirit goes. This means that while Paul is preaching to the Gentiles, the Holy Spirit is with him, and while Peter is ministering to the Jews in Jerusalem, the Holy Spirit is with him, simultaneously.

I want to take a brief detour to talk about the temple and tabernacle. We have already established that God desired to dwell with His people; this is evident in Eden. As we have discussed at length, between humanity and God stands the massive chasm of sin. God establishes the system of the tabernacle and the temple to address this divide. The first tabernacle instituted was the tabernacle of Moses, and within that tabernacle, there were three separate areas: the outer courts, the Holy Place, and the Holy of Holies, with each sphere getting closer to the manifest presence of God. The Jews could be in the outer courts where sacrifices were offered, but only priests could enter the Holy Place. Yet, your average run-of-the-mill priest wasn't allowed in the Holy of Holies; that sphere was reserved for the manifest presence of God and the High Priest, and even the High Priest could only enter one day a year. The Israelites could see the presence of God through a pillar of fire and the cloud by day but never *experienced* that presence up close.

Fast-forward, and Solomon replaces the tabernacle with an enormous, gaudy temple. I would also add that nowhere in Scripture do we see God initiating the changes Solomon makes; the adjustments seem to be the result of sheer hubris. Nevertheless, God fills the Holy of Holies with His presence. After generations of persistent sin, God uses Babylon to bring judgment upon Israel, resulting in the destruction of the temple and, contrary to what Indiana Jones might teach you, presumably the Ark of the Covenant.

Seventy years later, some Jews return to Jerusalem and rebuild the temple, but this time, there is no mention of the presence of God returning. It seems the Holy of Holies is empty.

A few hundred years later, Herod the Great builds an even more opulent temple, yet still, there is no mention of the presence of God returning. Author and theologian Daniel Hays posits that the presence of God did not return to the temple until Jesus Himself graced the temple with His presence. *"Jesus comes to Israel as the return of the presence of God."*[86]

When Jesus walked in, the presence of God returned.

Let's consider the purpose of the temple. The Temple was designed to be the nexus between God and humanity. John's gospel opens with,

> In the beginning was the Word, and the Word was with God, and the Word was God. He was in the beginning with God.... And the Word became flesh and dwelt among us. (John 1:1-2, 14, ESV)

---

86    J. Daniel Hays, *"The Temple and the Tabernacle"*, (Grand Rapids, MI: Baker Books, 2016), 166.

The word *dwelt* is the word "*tabernacled*". One commentator suggests, "*The allusion is to that tabernacle where dwelt the Shekinah…, or manifested 'GLORY OF THE LORD,' and with reference to God's permanent dwelling among His people.*"[87] In other words, with Jesus came the ultimate culmination of the tangible presence experienced at Moses' Tabernacle and Solomon's Temple.

Jesus saw Himself and taught that He was the new temple. In John 2, after Jesus cleanses the temple, the religious leaders ask by what authority He does all He does, and Jesus replies, "*Destroy this temple, and in three days I will raise it up.*" (John 2:19, ESV) When Jesus said '*temple*,' he meant *His body*.[88] In another place, Jesus most likely refers to Himself when He says, "*I tell you, something greater than the temple is here.*" (Matt. 12:6, ESV) The temple's purpose was to connect humanity with its Creator; Jesus was the fulfillment and the ultimate connection between man and his Creator.

When Jesus ascended to heaven, He tagged in the Holy Spirit, and now, through the Holy Spirit, *we are* the temple of God. His very presence dwells in us. Paul writes, "*Do you not know that your bodies are temples of the Holy Spirit, who is in you, whom you have received from God? You are not your own; you*

---

87    Robert Jamieson, A. R. Fausset, and David Brown, *Commentary Critical and Explanatory on the Whole Bible*, vol. 2 (Oak Harbor, WA: Logos Research Systems, Inc., 1997), 128.

88    "Clearly Jesus was speaking of himself as the *temple*, a new kind of temple." Donald Guthrie, "John," in *New Bible Commentary: 21st Century Edition*, ed. D. A. Carson et al., 4th ed. (Leicester, England; Downers Grove, IL: Inter-Varsity Press, 1994), 1030.

*were bought at a price. Therefore honor God with your bodies."*
(1 Cor. 6:19-20, NIV)

B.    The Holy Spirit Leads to Truth

In the social media age, truth can be hard to find. I'm writing this right after the 2024 US Presidential Election, and let me tell you, trying to figure out what was true seemed impossible at times. Part of the Holy Spirit's role is to lead believers to what is eternally true; namely, Jesus' teaching and identity.

Jesus will be glorified.

His teaching brought to remembrance.

He will guide us into *"all truth."*

Augustine is credited with saying, *"All truth is God's truth"* because God is the source of all truth. This is why John, in his first epistle, can say,

> *I write these things to you about those who are trying to deceive you. But the anointing that you received from him abides in you, and you have no need that anyone should teach you. But as his anointing teaches you about everything, and is true, and is no lie—just as it has taught you, abide in him.* (1 John 2:26-27, ESV)

John is not diminishing the importance of sound, biblical instruction. Rather, he is countering false teachers while affirming that the Spirit of God will guide believers toward truth and caution them against deception.

### C. The Holy Spirit Convicts

Jesus says the Holy Spirit will come to convict the world about sin, righteousness, and judgment.

J. Gresham Machen wrote a book called *"Christianity & Liberalism"* in 1923. He wrote it to address liberal Christianity, which was a discipline attempting to divorce Jesus from His divine nature. It enjoyed the moral teachings of Jesus but not the divine demand for repentance. Machen writes,

> *Modern liberalism has lost all sense of the gulf that separates the creature from the Creator…At the very root of the modern liberal movement is the loss of the consciousness of sin.*[89]

We have discussed this at length above, but we are sinners in desperate need of a Savior. I want to draw attention to the threefold conviction that Jesus highlights: the Holy Spirit convicts of sin, righteousness, and judgment. He elaborates on this, saying,

> *The world's sin is that it refuses to believe in me. Righteousness is available because I go to the Father, and you will see me no more. Judgment will come because the ruler of this world has already been judged.* (John 16:9-11, NLT)

Thus, the Holy Spirit's conviction starts by revealing our sin, then gently speaks to our souls the truth about Jesus' identity, urging us to turn in repentance. The Holy Spirit then points out that righteousness is available through the work of Jesus yet holds in tension the reality of eternal judgment.

---

[89]    J. Gresham Machen, *"Christianity & Liberalism"*, (Louisville, KY: GLH Publishing, 1923) 47.

We follow Jesus by following the indwelling leading of the Holy Spirit, who leads us to truth and is faithful to give us the gift of conviction. The Holy Spirit convicts us, points out the error of our ways, and invites us to respond.

### D. The Holy Spirit Empowers

In covering denial of self, bearing one's cross, and following Jesus, it is vital to understand that *none* of this can be done apart from the infilling power of the Holy Spirit. It is the Holy Spirit that gives us both the desire and power to live a changed life. Jesus promises in Acts, "*But you will receive power when the Holy Spirit has come upon you, and you will be my witnesses in Jerusalem and in all Judea and Samaria, and to the end of the earth.*" (Acts 1:8, ESV) Jesus, in promising the infilling of the Holy Spirit, specifically describes Him as infusing believers with power.

Power to witness.

Power to evangelize.

And as expounded in the New Testament, the power to live holy.

In Romans, Paul talks about *how* we put sin to death in our lives,

> *For if you live according to the flesh, you will die; but if by the Spirit you put to death the misdeeds of the body, you will live.* (Rom. 8:13, NIV)

In his letter to the Galatians, Paul juxtaposes the Fruit of the Flesh and the Fruit of the Spirit. He describes the Fruit of the

Flesh, that is, living according to our sinful nature, as,

> ...the works of the flesh are evident: sexual immorality, impurity, sensuality, idolatry, sorcery, enmity, strife, jealousy, fits of anger, rivalries, dissensions, divisions, envy, drunkenness, orgies, and things like these. I warn you, as I warned you before, that those who do such things will not inherit the kingdom of God. (Gal. 5:19-21, ESV)

When we give in to what is "natural", that is what our sinful nature craves; we will not inherit God's kingdom. The Holy Spirit and the Holy Spirit alone produces fruit that pleases God. As Paul says,

> So I say, walk by the Spirit, and you will not gratify the desires of the flesh...But the fruit of the Spirit is love, joy, peace, forbearance, kindness, goodness, faithfulness, gentleness and self-control. Against such things there is no law. Those who belong to Christ Jesus have crucified the flesh with its passions and desires. Since we live by the Spirit, let us keep in step with the Spirit. (Gal. 5:16,22-25, NIV)

Consider the illustration Paul uses. Produce.

One tree bears the fruit of sin, while the other yields the fruit of righteousness. Each of us must choose under which tree we will take refuge. If we want the Spirit's fruit, we need to be full of the Spirit. The more time you spend with the Holy Spirit, the more you produce love and joy, and peace, and patience, and kindness, and goodness, and faithfulness, and gentleness, and self-control.

The only way to deny the self, carry your cross, and follow Jesus is by the Spirit. In and of ourselves, we do not have the power or desire to live holy. But through the Holy Spirit, victory can be had. It is impossible to live a godly life that is not empowered by and fueled by the person of the Holy Spirit. To be clear, no amount of self-discipline or asceticism or mental fortitude can produce holiness.

Walking with the Spirit is to live in a way that feeds our redeemed Spiritual nature. Practically, this looks like the spiritual disciplines: Bible reading, prayer, worship, godly community, fasting, solitude, serving, and generosity, to name a few.

Through the power of the Holy Spirit, we're changed, moment by moment, day by day, closer and closer into the image of Jesus.

> *Now the Lord is the Spirit, and where the Spirit of the Lord is, there is freedom. And we all, with unveiled face, beholding the glory of the Lord, are being transformed into the same image from one degree of glory to another. For this comes from the Lord, who is the Spirit.* (2 Cor. 3:17-18, ESV)

### 2.    Through the Body of Christ

I mentioned this above and will go there again. Dietrich Bonhoeffer brilliantly said, *"Though we all have to enter upon discipleship alone, we do not remain alone."*[90] We must individually decide to follow Jesus, to die to our sins, and to surrender to His Lordship. However, when God saves us, He adopts us. When He adopts you, He places you into a family.

---

90    Bonhoeffer, *The Cost of Discipleship, 101.*

That family is His church.

The Christian faith is not one of rugged individualism but of codependent, coexisting members who belong to the same body. Paul stresses this truth in almost every one of his epistles.

> *Just as our bodies have many parts and each part has a special function, so it is with Christ's body. We are many parts of one body, and we all belong to each other.* (Romans 12:4-5, NLT)

> *For just as the body is one and has many members, and all the members of the body, though many, are one body, so it is with Christ. For in one Spirit we were all baptized into one body—Jews or Greeks, slaves or free—and all were made to drink of one Spirit* (1 Corinthians 12:12-13, ESV)

> *God has put all things under the authority of Christ and has made him head over all things for the benefit of the church. And the church is his body; it is made full and complete by Christ, who fills all things everywhere with himself.* (Ephesians 1:22-23, NLT)

> *And he is the head of the body, the church; he is the beginning and the firstborn from among the dead, so that in everything he might have the supremacy.* (Colossians 1:18, NIV)

God has not called individuals to isolationist spirituality but to an interconnected, interdependent familial community. Again, every time we see Jesus call an individual to follow Him, He calls them to follow Him *together*.

The call of Jesus comes to individuals, but obedience requires community.

Peter followed Jesus with James and John and Judas.

Together, they followed Jesus.

We accept the call of Jesus individually, but we follow Jesus collectively.

This theology exists in stark contrast to the expressive individualism promulgated by society. Rugged individualism, pull-yourself-up-by-your-bootstraps-ism, self-made men cannot exist in the Kingdom of God.

There have been times in my life when I have been insatiably desperate to hear God's voice. I fasted, prayed, jumped into the Word, and it still felt like the heavens were closed. God was seemingly uninterested in the happenings of my life. That is, until I got around some other people. What I failed to recognize was that God had chosen the unlikely vessels of other flawed, messed-up individuals to speak directly into my situation.

Could it be that in settling for isolation, you are cutting yourself off from hearing the voice of God through others?

The voice of others brings correction, encouragement, direction, support, and love. By devolving into isolation, we effectively cut off an entire medium God *frequently* uses to minister.

When considering ecclesiology, that is, the doctrine of the Church, it is important to define what the church is. When we think of church in the West, we think of a building, a 501(c)(3), an organization, a specific time, and a designated place. When God spoke of His church, He was talking about His people. His people, who had been called out of darkness, who had been rescued from death. His people that come from every walk of life, yet are bonded together through something more profound than familial bloodlines or melanin content. His people who have been united through the shed blood of Jesus.

His church, His people, are the very vehicle by which grace is distributed to a dying world, the fragrance by which communities smell Jesus, the arms by which the lonely are embraced, the feet by which the Gospel is carried, and the heartbeat of God in bodily form.

His people are broken and being mended. Sinful and being made holy. Squandered and being redeemed. His people, His congregation, His Church is the very thing He laid His life down to establish, and He is still the foreman overseeing its construction. For us in the 21st century to look down our noses at the supposed primitive nature of organized religion, thinking we have reached a more sophisticated, individual brand of Christianity, is a farce. It is a lie. It is a heretical notion.

God isn't building self-made people; He is building His family.

To follow Jesus requires following Him with others who have said "*yes*" to the same invitation.

## Line in the Sand

There are two paths: we follow Jesus, or we don't. We are in or we are out. Jesus laid down the requirements and definition of what it meant to be a disciple. To be a disciple requires a denial of self, a crucifixion of sin, and a continual, daily determination to follow Jesus, no matter where that may lead.

For the disciples, this was literal, and in the first century, to be a disciple was an honor. Between the ages of six and twelve, Jewish boys would begin a stage of schooling called *Beit Talmud*, which means "*House of the Book*". This first stage focused on memorizing the Torah: the first five books of the Bible. The students who showed the most promise had the opportunity to move on to advanced study, known as *Beit Sefer*, which translates to "*House of Learning.*" In this stage, the educational focus broadened to include the Law, the Prophets, the Writings, and the oral tradition. Those who showed enough promise could move on to *Beit Midrash*, meaning "*House of Study*". Beit Midrash included fierce debate on the application of Torah, which is one of the reasons Jesus was often involved in heated debates with the religious leaders.

More importantly, during Beit Midrash, students had the opportunity to become disciples of a rabbi. Students who showed enough aptitude could seek out a rabbi they admired, someone whose application of Scripture resonated with their soul. After applying to be a disciple, a student would enter an intensive interview process conducted by that rabbi. The interview encompassed everything from Scripture quotation and memorization to the application of the oral tradition to Jewish religious history. If the student passed the test, he would become a disciple.

That disciple committed to lifelong learning and following of his rabbi. He went where his rabbi went, dressed how he dressed, spoke like he spoke, interpreted Scripture like he interpreted Scripture, prayed like he prayed. To this day, among the ultra-orthodox in Jerusalem, you can identify which rabbi a Jewish man follows by his wardrobe.

One passage in the Mishnah from a teaching by Yose ben Yoezer says, *"Let your house be a meeting place for sages, sit in the dust at their feet, and drink in their words thirstily."*[91] It is believed that a famous blessing for disciples came from this passage. The blessing was simple: *"May the dust of your rabbi be upon you."*

May you follow your Rabbi so closely that the dust from his feet covers you.

This entire book was written to that end. I pray that you follow Jesus so closely that His dust is upon you.

Following Jesus requires death; we die to ourselves, we crucify our sins, and we choose, daily, to set our focus on God's will.

Following Jesus is difficult, yet, in the words of Robin Sharma, *"All change is hard at first, messy in the middle, and gorgeous at the end."*[92]

Following Jesus, though difficult, is the only true path to human flourishing. Leave all else behind, submit to His Lordship. Follow Jesus and in Him find true life.

---

91    Mishnah, Pirkei Avot 1:4, in *The Mishnah: A New Translation*, trans. Jacob Neusner (New Haven: Yale University Press, 1988), 37.

92    Robin Sharma, *The 5 AM Club: Own Your Morning, Elevate Your Life* (Carlsbad, CA: HarperCollins Leadership, 2018), 197.

# conclusion

———————

*"The call to discipleship, the baptism
in the name of Jesus Christ means both
death and life."*

**— Dietrich Bonhoeffer**

Life, hope, and flourishing. The invitation to follow Jesus is an act of grace. God, in His mercy, has offered a path of salvation. We come to Jesus because we desperately need life. That divine life produced within us generates eternal hope. Then, as an added bonus, we have the opportunity to truly flourish in this life.

Yet, flourishing is on the other side of denying oneself, living the crucified life, and choosing to follow Jesus, no matter where that may lead.

The temptation we face is to flip the order. Too many follow Jesus because they see Christianity as the newest attempt at flourishing; it is a spiritual self-help program.

If we pursue Jesus solely for flourishing in this life, we'll face deep disappointment when reality doesn't unfold as a carefree stroll through a field of daisies.

When we come to grips with the enormity of the chasm between us and a holy God and we see salvation as spiritual resuscitation first and foremost, then the uncertainty that comes will not thwart our discipleship.

We follow Jesus for Jesus, not for His stuff.

As we close this book, I want to end by reflecting on the goodness of Jesus. When considering discipleship as described by Jesus, a cost is involved. In fact, it costs us everything to follow Him.

We can't earn or pay for salvation; Jesus did that. But, in response to what He has done, He wants everything. Paul says it this way,

*You do not belong to yourself, for God bought you with a high price. So you must honor God with your body.* (1 Corinthians 6:19-20, NLT)

Paul is specifically addressing sexual immorality in this passage, yet the theology of ownership rings true. Jesus bought us with His blood; He owns us.

If you were to examine your discipleship honestly, is it obvious that you have been purchased by Jesus?

To live in a way that demonstrates Jesus' ownership requires sacrifice, and it's painful; the flesh doesn't want to die. Yet, the only way to flourish is to embrace that pain and bring it before Jesus.

My pastor, Dave Patterson, preached a brilliant message, and his closing line has stuck with me ever since. As he closed the message, he leaned in and said, *"Only at the cross do our ashes have value."*

Life creates ashes. Whether you live for Jesus or yourself, there will be some ashes. Pain is a part of the human experience. Yet, only at the cross, only in running to Jesus, can the ashes of our lives be turned into something beautiful, something extraordinary. He is the God of the exchange.

He exchanges our sin for righteousness.

He exchanges our death for life.

He exchanges wandering for hope.

He exchanges confusion for flourishing.

Yes, there is pain involved in discipleship. Discipleship costs you everything. But in light of the beauty of Jesus, when considering His love, His mercy, His grace, His kindness, the simple reality of who He is, the cost is nothing.

When Jesus saved me, I was a depressed, suicidal, two-faced pastor's kid. I was a liar, a manipulator; I worked people for my benefit. I used *the church* to benefit me and my sinful lifestyle. And in that place, the grace of Jesus met me, wooed me, the Holy Spirit convicted me, and the moment of decision was presented.

When I consider the mercy and grace of God I have experienced in the fifteen years since then, the cost of discipleship pales in comparison.

Jesus is better.

He invited me to find life, so I came close.

He invited me to experience true hope, so I continue to draw near.

He has laid out the path to true flourishing, and I endeavor to die each day.

This whole book can be summarized in this awkward sentence:

> *We are dead and need to be made alive.*
> *Then, to truly live, we need to die.*

So, have you come to Him?

Are you in the process of dying?

In the words of Jesus, "*If you try to hang on to your life, you will lose it. But if you give up your life for my sake, you will save it.*" (Luke 9:24, NLT)

To *Come and Die* is an invitation to embrace a 2,000-year-old way of life—an ancient path that leads to life, hope, and flourishing. Though clearly marked, this path is narrow, and few are willing to walk it. Stepping onto it is simple in principle, yet profoundly difficult in practice. To journey down this road—to face its dangers, endure its trials, and press toward its end—is to discover what it means to truly live.

Let's close this book the way we began it, with Dietrich Bonhoeffer, who was called "*a giant before man, was but a child before God.*"[93] I leave you with two quotes: may you endeavor to come to Jesus, die to yourself, experience life, and that life to the full.

> *We can only achieve perfect liberty and enjoy fellowship with Jesus when his command, his call to absolute discipleship is appreciated in its entirety. Only the man who follows the command of Jesus single-mindedly, and unresistingly lets his yoke rest upon him, finds his burden easy, and under its gentle pressure receives the power to persevere in the right way. The command of Jesus is hard, unutterably hard, for those who try to resist it. But for those who willingly submit, the yoke is easy, and the burden light. "His commands are not grievous." (1 John 5:3)*[94]

---

93    Bonhoeffer, *The Cost of Discipleship*, 19

94    Bonhoeffer, *The Cost of Discipleship*, 37.

*Only Jesus Christ, who bids us follow him, knows the journey's end. But we do know that it will be a road of boundless mercy. Discipleship means joy.*[95]

---

95    Bonhoeffer, *The Cost of Discipleship*, 38.

appendix:
# hell and judgment

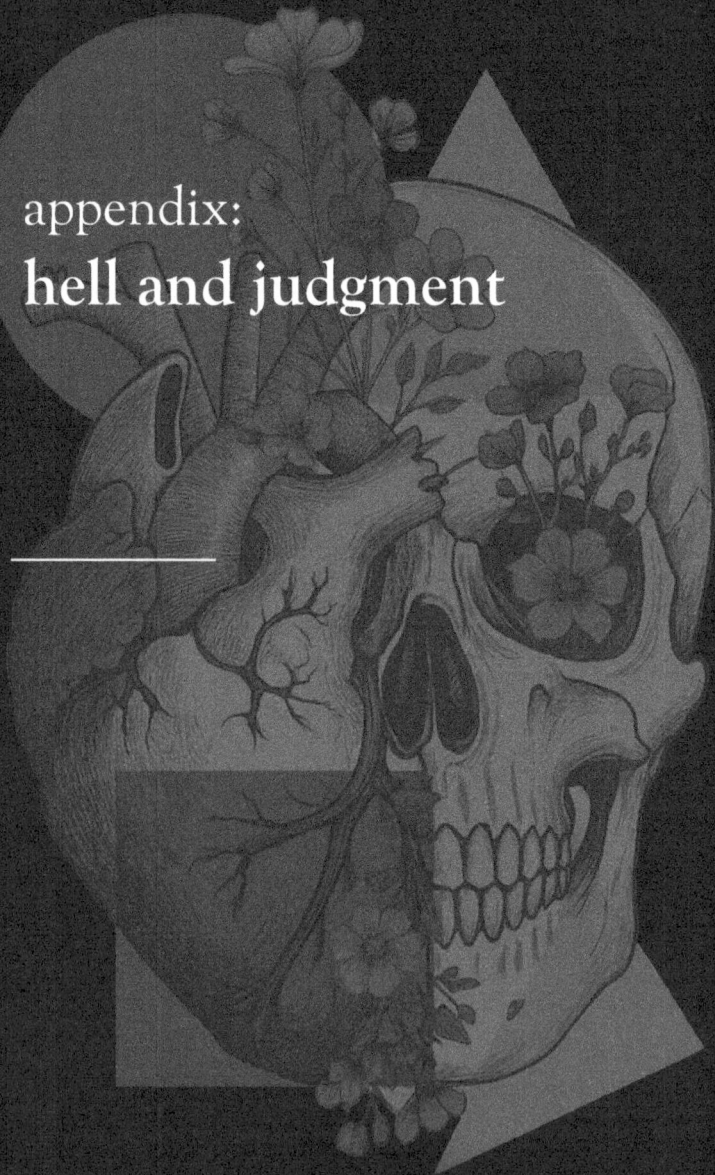

_____

The primary purpose of this book is to guide believers in pursuing genuine discipleship. So, I didn't feel it was necessary to devote an entire chapter to hell or eternal judgment, though both are referenced multiple times throughout. However, I felt it would be incomplete not to address both concepts in an appendix. So, here we are. This appendix aims to outline a grounded theology of hell and eternal judgment. This section will not be all-inclusive but will hopefully cover the "basics".

## 1.    Judgment

Throughout the book, I discussed the dichotomies in Scripture. Those dichotomies extend to the very character of God.

God is love and has perfect wrath.

God is kind yet hates sin.

God is merciful yet perfectly just.

Now, to be clear, *all* of these characteristics are true and can be easily reconciled.

For example, I am a father, and I love my kids. There is nothing on this planet I would not do for them. Because I love my kids, if you harm them, you will experience my utter and complete wrath. True love has true wrath.

In this same vein, because God is the *embodiment* of truth, He must be perfect justice. Justice is what happens when truth wins.

I've heard it said that "*at the cross, the perfect love and perfect wrath of God meet.*" In the brutality of the cross, God's wrath was poured out. In Jesus' vicarious execution for all who would believe, His love is seen. 2 Corinthians plainly states, *"God made him who had no sin to be sin for us, so that in him we might become the righteousness of God."* (2 Cor. 5:21, NIV)

The reality of sin demands payment; that payment is either paid by us in eternity or by Jesus at the Cross. For those who submit to the Lordship of Jesus, their debt has been paid by Christ Himself. For those who refuse Christ's sacrifice, their bill will come due.

God, being perfect justice, must penalize sin. A.W. Tozer observed, *"Justice is not something that God has. Justice is something that God is."*[96] Though evil exists on this planet now, it will all *ultimately* be made right. D.A. Carson wrote, *"The Bible insists that God is entirely just, and that therefore ultimately justice will be done, and will be seen to be done."*[97]

The Bible clearly teaches an end-time judgment where every person who has ever existed must stand before Jesus and give an account of their life.

> *For God will bring every deed into judgment, with every secret thing, whether good or evil.* (Ecclesiastes 12:14, ESV)
>
> *I tell you, on the day of judgment people will give account for every careless word they speak, for by your words you*

---

96   A.W. Tozer, The Attributes of God, ed. David F. Edwards (Camp Hill, PA: Christian Publications, 1997), 60.

97   D. A. Carson, quoted in John Blanchard, *The Complete Gathered Gold: A Treasury of Quotations for Christians* (Ross-shire, Scotland: Christian Focus Publications, 2006), 362–63.

*will be justified, and by your words you will be condemned.*
(Matthew 12:36-37, ESV)

*The times of ignorance God overlooked, but now he commands all people everywhere to repent, because he has fixed a day on which he will judge the world in righteousness by a man whom he has appointed; and of this he has given assurance to all by raising him from the dead."* (Acts 17:30-31, ESV)

*But because of your hard and impenitent heart you are storing up wrath for yourself on the day of wrath when God's righteous judgment will be revealed. He will render to each one according to his works: to those who by patience in well-doing seek for glory and honor and immortality, he will give eternal life; but for those who are self-seeking and do not obey the truth, but obey unrighteousness, there will be wrath and fury.* (Romans 2:5-8, ESV)

*For we must all appear before the judgment seat of Christ, so that each one may receive what is due for what he has done in the body, whether good or evil.* (2 Corinthians 5:10, ESV)

*And just as it is appointed for man to die once, and after that comes judgment...* (Hebrews 9:27, ESV)

*Then I saw a great white throne and him who was seated on it. From his presence, earth and sky fled away, and no place was found for them. And I saw the dead, great and small, standing before the throne, and books were opened. Then another book was opened, which is the book of life. And the dead were judged by what was written in the books, according to what they had done.* (Revelation 20:11-12, ESV)

Throughout this book, I have argued that Jesus calls us to follow Him individually, and then we do the actual *following* collectively. At judgment, it's back to individuality. Each of us must stand before Jesus alone. We are either seen through the lens of the Cross of Christ, where the penalty for sin is paid in full, standing in Christ's righteousness, or we stand alone in our righteousness, which is *"filthy rags."*[98]. Essentially, the questions asked at the judgment are:

1.   What did you do with Jesus? [99]

2.   How did you steward your life?

If the answer to the first question isn't complete repentance and surrender to his Lordship, then the answer to the second question doesn't matter.

Theologian Kevin Connor wrote,

> *The Scriptures teach that man is on probation during his time on earth. Those who respond to God's grace and obey Him will be eternally rewarded in heaven, God's dwelling place. Those who willfully resist the grace of God, do their own will, and serve Satan will be eternally punished in hell, Satan's dwelling place. Eternal destinies are settled here in time.*[100]

The experience of "the judgement" is not the same for everyone. Jesus clearly states,

---

98   Is.64:6.

99   By this I mean what did you believe about who Jesus is and did you submit your life to His Lordship.

100   Kevin J. Conner, *The Foundations of Christian Doctrine*, (Portland, OR; City Christian Publishing, 1982)293.

*Do not marvel at this, for an hour is coming when all who are in the tombs will hear his voice, and come out, those who have done good to the resurrection of life, and those who have done evil to the resurrection of judgment.* (John 5:28-29, ESV)

Jesus indicates that the Day of Judgment for believers is a day of *reward*. Jesus repeatedly speaks of God being a rewarding God; those rewards are distributed in eternity.[101] The aim for the disciple is to steward his life well. It is to hear those beautiful words,

*Well done, good and faithful servant. You have been faithful over a little; I will set you over much. Enter into the joy of your master.'* (Matt. 25:21, ESV)

## 2. Hell

Hell is not a popular concept in the 21st-century West. Yet, in its essence, hell is God giving people what they want. C.S. Lewis famously wrote,

"*The gates of hell are locked on the inside.*"[102]

"*There are only two kinds of people in the end: those who say to God, 'Thy will be done,' and those to whom God says, in the end, 'Thy will be done.'*"[103]

J.I. Packer agreed, writing, "*Scripture sees hell as self-chosen... the*

---

101  Matt.5:11-12; 6:1-20; 10:41-42; 16:27; 19:21-29 just to start.

102  C. S. Lewis, *The Problem of Pain* (New York: HarperOne, 2001), 130.

103  C. S. Lewis, *The Great Divorce* (New York: HarperOne, 2001), 72

*essence of God's judgment is to abandon people to themselves.*"[104] The late Tim Keller also concurred, "*Hell is simply one's freely chosen identity apart from God on a trajectory into infinity.*"[105]

Through the centuries, there have been a few predominant views of what hell is.

### 1. Annihilationism

This view of hell holds that God will judge the wicked, but after their judgment, they will be destroyed. Punishment is not for eternity but for a finite time. The primary verses that are used to support this view are:

- **Matthew 10:28** – "...fear him who can destroy both soul and body in hell."

- **Romans 6:23** – "For the wages of sin is death..."

- **John 3:16** – "...whoever believes in him should not perish..."

- **2 Peter 2:6** – "...turning the cities of Sodom and Gomorrah to ashes... making them an example of what is going to happen to the ungodly."

Theologian John Stott concluded, "*It would seem strange... if people who are said to suffer destruction are in fact not destroyed; and... it is difficult to imagine a perpetually inconclusive process*

---

104    J. I. Packer, *Evangelism and the Sovereignty of God* (Downers Grove, IL: InterVarsity Press, 1961), 138.

105    Timothy Keller, *The Reason for God: Belief in an Age of Skepticism* (New York: Dutton, 2008), 79.

*of perishing.*"[106] Additionally, Preston Sprinkle, a modern-day scholar, leans toward annihilationism. [107]

In sum, annihilation holds that God's judgment is final; He judges, condemns, and then destroys. Thus, hell essentially describes the destruction process.

### 2. Universal Reconciliation (Universalism)

This view holds that *all* people will eventually be reconciled to God, even if some experience postmortem salvation or purification. The primary verses that are used to support this view are:

- **1 Timothy 2:3-4** – "This is good, and it is pleasing in the sight of God our Savior, who desires all people to be saved..."

- **Philippians 2:10-11** – "...every knee should bow... every tongue confess that Jesus Christ is Lord..."

- **Colossians 1:20** – "...reconcile to himself all things..."

- **Romans 5:18** – "...one act of righteousness leads to justification and life for all men."

Some theologians who seem to lean into universal reconciliation were Karl Barth[108], Origen, and Gregory

---

106   John R. W. Stott, quoted in David L. Edwards and John R. W. Stott, *Evangelical Essentials: A LiberalEvangelical Dialogue* (Leicester, UK: InterVarsity Press, 1988), 314–15.

107   Preston Sprinkle, "Is Annihilation an Evangelical Option?" *Preston Sprinkle Blog,* February 3, 2015.

108    Karl Barth, *Church Dogmatics*, vol. 4/1: *The Doctrine of Reconciliation Part 1*, trans. G. W. Bromiley (Edinburgh: T&T Clark, 1956), 91–92.

of Nyssa. Gregory of Nyssa wrote, *"Evil must be altogether removed, and all must be made subject to God... until every created being is brought into the same condition as before the fall."*[109]Centuries earlier, Origen wrote, *"All souls... shall be restored sooner or later to God's friendship. The evolution will be long... but a time will come when God shall be all in all."*[110]

Essentially, Universal reconciliation is the theological view that, in the end, all people—including those who die in unbelief or without repentance—will ultimately be reconciled to God and receive salvation. This view challenges the traditional doctrine of eternal damnation, asserting that God's love, mercy, and justice will prevail to restore every soul to Himself.

3. Eternal Conscious Torment

Against these two views stands the traditional view of hell as a state of eternal, conscious torment. In my view, this perspective carries the most biblical weight and appears to align most clearly with Jesus' teaching. The view of eternal conscious torment posits that hell is a literal place or state of eternal punishment where the souls of the unrighteous endure unending conscious agony, separated from God. Unlike annihilationism (which posits the wicked are destroyed) or universal reconciliation (which anticipates eventual salvation for all), this view emphasizes the permanence of punishment, reflecting God's holiness and justice.

---

109 Gregory of Nyssa, *The Great Catechism*, ch. 26, in *Nicene and Post-Nicene Fathers, Second Series*, vol. 5, ed. Schaff and Wace, 5:416.

110 Origen, *On First Principles*, book III, chp. 6, sec. 6, in *Ante-Nicene Fathers*, vol. 4.

First, this perspective asserts that hell was intended not for human beings, but for Satan and his demons, the original agents of sin. Jesus, when teaching about judgment, said, "*Then he will say to those on his left, 'Depart from me, you cursed, into the eternal fire prepared for the devil and his angels.*" (Matt. 25:41, ESV) Once humanity sinned, they became deserving of the same punishment as Satan.

Second, hell is eternal separation from God. I can say that "*hell is God giving people what they want*" because those who choose to live apart from God in this life ultimately receive what they pursued—an eternity separated from Him. Paul phrases it like this to the church in Thessaloniki,

> … *when the Lord Jesus is revealed from heaven with his mighty angels in flaming fire, inflicting vengeance on those who do not know God and on those who do not obey the gospel of our Lord Jesus. They will suffer the punishment of eternal destruction, away from the presence of the Lord and from the glory of his might…* (2 Thessalonians 1:7b-9, ESV)

To explain eternal, conscious torment, let's examine the words of Jesus. Of all the New Testament voices, Jesus spoke the most plainly about the reality of hell. When referring to '*hell*', Jesus used two different Greek words.

1.  Hades

Jesus uses the term '*Hades*' four times to describe hell. In Greek mythology, Hades (also called Pluto) was originally the god of the underworld. His realm took on his name and was believed to be the realm of the dead. In a sense, it was the Greek equivalent of '*Sheol*'. Like Sheol, all the dead went to Hades, not just the wicked. It has been noted, "*Originally the Greeks thought of Hades as simply the grave, a shadowy, ghostlike existence that happened to all who died, good and evil alike.*" [111] That belief gradually changed as Hades itself was divided into three primary areas: Elysium (paradise for the virtuous), the Asphodel Meadows (a neutral place for ordinary souls, and Tartarus (a deep pit to punish the wicked). In Greek mythology, judgment took place after death. The souls of the dead were ferried across the River Styx by Charon and then judged. Their final destination within Hades depended on their moral conduct and favor with the gods. Hades itself was not "hell" in the modern sense, but rather the general realm of the dead, containing distinct areas for both reward and punishment.

By the time of the translation of the Septuagint, the translators used the term '*Hades*' to translate '*Sheol*'. Jews progressively began to believe in the resurrection of the dead, the rewarding of the righteous, and the punishment of the wicked in eternity. As Peter Davids observes, "*by the beginning of the NT period Hades has three meanings: (1) death, (2) the place of all the dead, and (3) the place of the wicked dead only.*" [112]

---

111   Peter H. Davids, "Hades," in *Baker Encyclopedia of the Bible* (Grand Rapids, MI: Baker Book House, 1988), 912.

112   Peter H. Davids, "Hades," in *Baker Encyclopedia of the Bible* (Grand Rapids, MI: Baker Book House, 1988), 912.

First-century Jewish tradition often viewed Hades as a "holding place" for the dead until the time of eternal judgment.

When Jesus used the term Hades, context determines which meaning He was referring to. In Matthew 11 and Luke 10, Jesus pronounces ruin to three cities that have rejected Him,

> *And you, Capernaum, will you be exalted to heaven? You will be brought down to Hades. For if the mighty works done in you had been done in Sodom, it would have remained until this day.* (Matthew 11:23, ESV)

In this context, Jesus is describing the judgment that will befall Capernaum for their rejection of His message and ministry.

In Matthew 16, Jesus famously declares that He will build His church and *"the gates of hell (Hades) shall not prevail against it."* (Matt. 16:18, ESV) One scholar describes this usage, saying, *"The gates of Hades is a poetic expression for death; this new community of those who follow Jesus will never die."*[113] Jesus is describing the eternal nature of His Kingdom and the advancement of His Church. Death itself could not prevent the progressive movement of His Kingdom in and through His Church. [114]

---

113    Richard T. France, "Matthew," in *New Bible Commentary: 21st Century Edition*, ed. D. A. Carson et al., 4th ed. (Leicester, England; Downers Grove, IL: Inter-Varsity Press, 1994), 926.

114    Robert Jamieson, A. R. Fausset, and David Brown, *Commentary Critical and Explanatory on the Whole Bible*, vol. 2 (Oak Harbor, WA: Logos Research Systems, Inc., 1997), 48.

## 2.    Gehenna

Whereas Hades was mainly seen as a holding tank for the dead, Gehenna was used to describe eternal judgment. Gehenna is a Greek translation for the *Valley of Hinnom*, a ravine south of Jerusalem. In the Old Testament, the Valley of Hinnom is described as a place where Israel engaged in idolatry, child sacrifice, and wickedness.

> *And they have built the high places of Topheth, which is in the Valley of the Son of Hinnom, to burn their sons and their daughters in the fire, which I did not command, nor did it come into my mind.* (Jeremiah 7:31, ESV)

> *…therefore, behold, days are coming, declares the LORD, when this place shall no more be called Topheth, or the Valley of the Son of Hinnom, but the Valley of Slaughter.* (Jeremiah 19:6, ESV)

> *Ahaz was twenty years old when he began to reign, and he reigned sixteen years in Jerusalem. And he did not do what was right in the eyes of the LORD, as his father David had done, but he walked in the ways of the kings of Israel. He even made metal images for the Baals, and he made offerings in the Valley of the Son of Hinnom and burned his sons as an offering, according to the abominations of the nations whom the Lord drove out before the people of Israel.* (2 Chronicles 28:1-3, ESV)

According to tradition, either the Ammonites, King Ahaz, or Manasseh[115] constructed a bronze statue of Molech,

---

115   The Jerusalem Talmud and Babylonian Talmud attribute the statue to the Ammonites while later commentaries suggest King Ahaz or King Manasseh constructed it.

portrayed as a bull-headed figure with outstretched arms. A fire was kindled at the base of the statue, and worshippers would place infants into its arms, allowing them to fall into the flames. Drums were beaten loudly by onlookers to muffle the children's cries.

This horrific scene led to Gehenna being slang for "*eternal judgment.*" By the intertestamental period, Jewish literature began to portray Gehenna not merely as a physical valley, but as a spiritual realm of judgment. Texts like *1 Enoch* and various books from the Apocrypha depict it as a place where the wicked are condemned, the ungodly are consumed by fire, and angels execute divine punishment. Similarly, rabbinic writings in the Mishnah and Talmud associate Gehenna with post-mortem punishment, which is sometimes viewed as temporary and at other times as eternal.

Jesus used Gehenna eleven times to speak of eternal, conscious torment. His audience understood that He was speaking of a *real*, horrific place that was used to describe a place of judgment. Jesus describes Gehenna, hell, this way,

> *And if your hand causes you to sin, cut it off. It is better for you to enter life crippled than with two hands to go to hell, to the unquenchable fire.* (Mark 9:43, ESV)

> *But I say to you that everyone who is angry with his brother will be liable to judgment; whoever insults his brother will be liable to the council; and whoever says, 'You fool!' will be liable to the hell of fire.* (Matthew 5:22, ESV)

*And do not fear those who kill the body but cannot kill the soul. Rather fear him who can destroy both soul and body in hell.* (Matthew 10:28, ESV)

*But I will warn you whom to fear: fear him who, after he has killed, has authority to cast into hell. Yes, I tell you, fear him!* (Luke 12:5, ESV)

*And if your eye causes you to sin, tear it out. It is better for you to enter the kingdom of God with one eye than with two eyes to be thrown into hell, 'where their worm does not die and the fire is not quenched.'* (Mark 9:47-48, ESV)

From these verses alone, Jesus teaches that:

1. Our actions lead to judgment, and Gehenna is connected to that

2. God sends people to Gehenna

3. Gehenna is destructive

4. Gehenna is a place of unquenchable fire

5. Nothing dies in Gehenna

In addition to Hades and Gehenna, Jesus uses a variety of metaphors and similes to describe eternal punishment. Jesus describes hell as:

- "Outer darkness"[116]

- "Weeping and gnashing of teeth"[117]

---

116 *Matthew 8:12; 22:13; 25:30*

117 *Matthew 13:42, 50; 24:51; Luke 13:28*

- "Unquenchable fire" / "Eternal fire"[118]
- "Furnace of fire"[119]
- "Destruction"[120]

Putting together everything Jesus said about hell, it's clear that He described it as a real and eternal place of punishment for the wicked. It is an eternal furnace that is eternally dark, and its inhabitants weep, gnash their teeth, and are tormented.

## The Rest of the New Testament

Outside of the words of Jesus in the Gospels, hell is described in the New Testament by Paul, in Hebrews, Peter, Jude, and Revelation. Paul opts to describe the final judgment. Reiterating what we covered earlier, he says in 1 Thessalonians,

> ...when the Lord Jesus is revealed from heaven with his mighty angels in flaming fire, inflicting vengeance on those who do not know God and on those who do not obey the gospel of our Lord Jesus. They will suffer the punishment of eternal destruction, away from the presence of the Lord and from the glory of his might... (1 Thessalonians 1:7b-9, ESV)

Notice, he highlights those who do not know God are subject to judgment, which is eternal punishment away from the presence of God. Some in the annihilationist camp believe this verse proves their belief due to Paul saying, "eternal *destruction.*" However, the Greek word used here for

---

118  *Mark 9:43; Matthew 18:8; 25:41*

119  *Matthew 13:42, 50*

120  *Matthew 7:13 (broad road leads to destruction)*

*destruction* is the word *olethros*, meaning "*an event or act that results in destruction; especially the loss of all that gives worth to existence.*" Paul is not referring to the erasure of existence; he is speaking of the erasure of purpose.

Paul describes hell and judgment in Romans, saying,

> But because of your hard and impenitent heart you are storing up wrath for yourself on the day of wrath when God's righteous judgment will be revealed. He will render to each one according to his works: to those who by patience in well-doing seek for glory and honor and immortality, he will give eternal life; but for those who are self-seeking and do not obey the truth, but obey unrighteousness, there will be wrath and fury. (Rom. 2:5-8, ESV)

Paul reiterates Jesus' teaching of eternal judgment according to how we steward our lives. God's judgment will be a demonstration of His righteous wrath and fury. This same sentiment is repeated in Hebrews.[121]

When Peter talks about hell, he mentions that it's where the fallen angels were sent[122] and highlights that Sodom and Gomorrah are "*an example of what is going to happen to the ungodly...*" (2 Peter 2:6b, NIV). Jude echoes this same sentiment[123] and adds that hell is "*utter darkness.*"[124]

---

121    Heb.10:26-27.

122    2 Pet. 2:4.

123    Jude 7.

124    Jude 13.

Revelation summarizes New Testament teaching on hell, stating,

> *And another angel, a third, followed them, saying with a loud voice, "If anyone worships the beast and its image and receives a mark on his forehead or on his hand, he also will drink the wine of God's wrath, poured full strength into the cup of his anger, and he will be tormented with fire and sulfur in the presence of the holy angels and in the presence of the Lamb. And the smoke of their torment goes up forever and ever, and they have no rest, day or night, these worshipers of the beast and its image, and whoever receives the mark of its name."* (Revelation 14:9-11, ESV)

> *…and the devil who had deceived them was thrown into the lake of fire and sulfur where the beast and the false prophet were, and they will be tormented day and night forever and ever. Then I saw a great white throne and him who was seated on it. From his presence earth and sky fled away, and no place was found for them. And I saw the dead, great and small, standing before the throne, and books were opened. Then another book was opened, which is the book of life. And the dead were judged by what was written in the books, according to what they had done. And the sea gave up the dead who were in it, Death and Hades gave up the dead who were in them, and they were judged, each one of them, according to what they had done. Then Death and Hades were thrown into the lake of fire. This is the second death, the lake of fire. And if anyone's name was not found written in the book of life, he was thrown into the lake of fire.* (Revelation 20:10-15, ESV)

The New Testament teaches that all humanity deserves judgment because of sin, and the punishment we rightly deserve is eternal separation from God. Yet, Jesus paid that penalty on the cross. We either accept His payment or we pay eternally in hell. Hell is eternal, conscious torment. It was designed for the first sinner, but when humanity engaged in the act of sin, we earned the same punishment.

Humans are immortal; we either live eternally with God or eternally apart from God. With God is *"fullness of joy....[and] pleasures forevermore."* (Ps. 16:11, ESV) Hell, a place void of God's presence, is a place void of all that is good because God is the source of good. Thus, hell is a place void of love, joy, peace, kindness, and pleasure.

Ultimately, every human being must stand before God and give an account of their life. My prayer is that we all accept Jesus' sacrifice and be found in Him on that day.

# acknowledgments

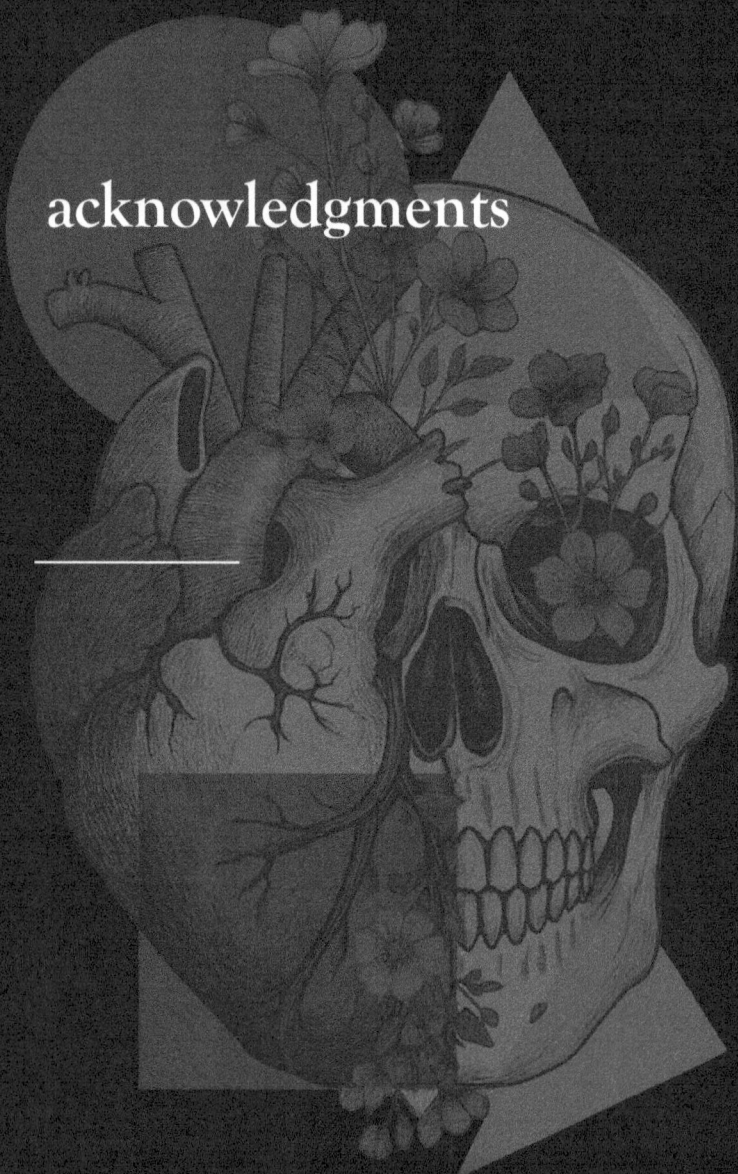

_____

I first want to thank my King, Jesus. You have brought me back to life.

Thank you to my wife, Rachel. You are my greatest cheerleader and the backbone of our family. I love you, boo thang.

Levi, Livvy, my babies, I love you. You are young now, but it is my goal, my highest aim, for you to experience everything in the preceding pages. That you would experience the bliss of knowing Jesus and identify with His death, burial, and resurrection.

Thank you to my family for a life of ministry and fun. Mom and Dad, thank you for demonstrating how to love Jesus, love your family, and serve the Church. You are the real MVP.

The Father's House, the greatest church on this planet. Thank you for bringing your mess to the foot of the Cross and embracing the call of discipleship. Thank you, Pastors Dave and Donna, for championing leaders and believing in people.

# bibliography

Athanasius of Alexandria, *On the Incarnation*, 27.3. Translated by John Behr. Yonkers, NY: St. Vladimir's Seminary Press, 2011.

Augustine of Hippo, *Confessions,* trans. Henry Chadwick, Oxford: Oxford University Press, 1991.

Augustine, *On the Trinity*, Book XIV, Chapter 15, in *The Nicene and Post-Nicene Fathers,* First Series, Vol. 3, ed. Philip Schaff, trans. Arthur West Haddan, Buffalo, NY: Christian Literature Publishing Co., 1887, reprinted in *The Early Church Fathers* series.

Ambrose, *On the Duties of the Clergy*, Book I, Chapter 13, in *Nicene and Post-Nicene Fathers, Second Series*, Vol. 10, ed. Philip Schaff and Henry Wace, trans. H. De Romestin, Buffalo, NY: Christian Literature Publishing Co., 1896, reprinted in *The Early Church Fathers* series.

Arndt, William et al., *A Greek-English Lexicon of the New Testament and Other Early Christian Literature*, Chicago: University of Chicago Press, 2000.

Barna Group, "Americans Draw Theological Beliefs From Diverse Points of View," *Barna*, October 8, 2002, https://www.barna.com/research/americans-draw-theological-beliefs-from-diverse-points-of-view/.

Barth, Karl, *Church Dogmatics*, vol. 4/1: *The Doctrine of Reconciliation Part 1*, trans. G. W. Bromiley, Edinburgh: T&T Clark, 1956.

Bonhoeffer, Dietrich, *The Cost of Discipleship,* New York; Touchstone, 1937.

Borland, Elizabeth. "Standpoint Theory." Encyclopedia Britannica. Accessed August 8, 2024. https://www.britannica.com/topic/standpoint-theory.

Brown, Brené, *Daring Greatly: How the Courage to Be Vulnerable Transforms the Way We Live, Love, Parent, and Lead*, New York: Gotham Books, 2012.

Calvin, John, *Commentaries on the Book of the Prophet Jeremiah and the Lamentations*, vol. 1, trans. John Owen, Edinburgh: Calvin Translation Society, 1850.

Campbell, David, *Landmarks*, Holland, MI: Unprecedented Press LLC, 2017.

Carrey, Jim, interview with Jay Stone, 2005, as cited in *AZ Quotes*,accessedSeptember2024,https://www.azquotes.com/quote/520133.

Chesterton, G.K., The Everlasting Man, San Francisco: Ignatius Press, 1993.

Clearview Treatment Programs, "*The Effects of Shame on Mental Health and Addiction Recovery*," Clearview Treatment,accessedSeptember2024,https://www.clearviewtreatment.com.

Comer, John Mark, *Garden City*, Grand Rapids: Zondervan, 2015.

Conner, Kevin J., Ken Malmin, *"New Testament Survey"*. Portland, OR; City Bible Publishing, 1975.
——*The Foundations of Christian Doctrine*, Portland, OR; City Christian Publishing, 1982.

Davids, Peter H., "Hades," in *Baker Encyclopedia of the Bible*, Grand Rapids, MI: Baker Book House, 1988.

Elwell, Walter A. and Barry J. Beitzel, "Heaven," *Baker Encyclopedia of the Bible*, Grand Rapids, MI: Baker Book House, 1988.

Fee, Gordon D. and Robert L. Hubbard Jr., eds., *The Eerdmans Companion to the Bible*, Grand Rapids, MI; Cambridge, U.K.: William B. Eerdmans Publishing Company, 2011.

Feinberg, Charles L., "Atonement, Day Of," *Baker Encyclopedia of the Bible*, Grand Rapids, MI: Baker Book House, 1988.

Flavius Josephus, *Antiquities of the Jews*, 18.1.3.—— *The Jewish War*, 2.8.14.

Fiensy, David A., "Crucifixion," ed. John D. Barry et al., *The Lexham Bible Dictionary*, Bellingham, WA: Lexham Press, 2016.

France, Richard T., "Matthew," in *New Bible Commentary: 21st Century Edition*, ed. D. A. Carson et al., 4th ed., Leicester, England; Downers Grove, IL: Inter-Varsity Press, 1994.

Gregory of Nyssa, *The Life of Moses*, Book II, in *The Classics of Western Spirituality* series, trans. Abraham J. Malherbe and Everett Ferguson, New York: Paulist Press, 1978.

—— *The Great Catechism*, ch. 26, in *Nicene and Post-Nicene Fathers, Second Series*, vol. 5, ed. Schaff and Wace, 5:416.

Harding, Sandra. "Introduction: Standpoint Theory as a Site of Political, Philosophic, and Scientific Debate" in *The Feminist Standpoint Theory Reader: Intellectual & Political Controversies*, 2004, New York and London: Routledge.

Hays, J. Daniel. "*The Temple and the Tabernacle*", Grand Rapids, MI: Baker Books, 2016.

Hobbes, Thomas. *"The Essential Leviathan: A Modernized Edition", Indianapolis*: Hackett Publishing, 2016.

Hume, David, *Dialogues Concerning Natural Religion*, ed. Richard H. Popkin, Indianapolis: Hackett Publishing, 1998.

Irenaeus, *Against Heresies*, Book IV, Chapter 20, Section 7, in *Ante-Nicene Fathers*, ed. Alexander Roberts and James Donaldson, trans. A. Cleveland Coxe, Buffalo, NY: Christian Literature Publishing Co., 1885, reprinted in *The Early Church Fathers* series.

Keller, Timothy, *Counterfeit Gods: The Empty Promises of Money, Sex, and Power, and the Only Hope That Matters*, New York: Dutton, 2009.

—— *The Reason for God: Belief in an Age of Skepticism*. New York: Dutton, 2008.

Kimball, Dan, *How (NOT) to Read the Bible*, Grand Rapids, MI: Zondervan, 2020.

Klein, William W., Craig L. Blomberg, Robert L. Hubbard, Jr., (*Introduction to Biblical Interpretation*, Nashville, TN: Thomas Nelson, INC, 2004.

Kruse, Colin G., "2 Corinthians," in *New Bible Commentary: 21st Century Edition*, ed. D. A. Carson et al., 4th ed., Leicester, England; Downers Grove, IL: Inter-Varsity Press, 1994.

Ladd, George E., "Kingdom of God (Heaven)," *Baker Encyclopedia of the Bible*, Grand Rapids, MI: Baker Book House, 1988.

Lightner, Robert P., "Philippians," in *The Bible Knowledge Commentary: An*

    *Exposition of the Scriptures*, ed. J. F. Walvoord and R. B. Zuck, vol. 2, Wheaton, IL: Victor Books, 1985.

Lewis, C.S., *Mere Christianity*, New York: HarperCollins, 2001.
    —— *The Great Divorce* (New York: HarperOne, 2001), 72
    —— *The Problem of Pain* (New York: HarperOne, 2001), 130.

Luther, Martin, *The Large Catechism*, in *Luther's Works*, vol. 38, ed. Helmut T. Lehmann, Philadelphia: Fortress Press, 1959.

MacGregor, Kirk R., "Mark, Gospel of," ed. John D. Barry et al., *The Lexham Bible Dictionary*, Bellingham, WA: Lexham Press, 2016.

Machen, J. Gresham, "*Christianity & Liberalism*", Louisville, KY: GLH Publishing, 1923.

Malina, Bruce J. *The New Testament World: Insights from Cultural Anthropology.* Louisville, KY.: Westminster John Knox, 1981.

Matthews, Victor H. "Making Your Point: The Use of Gestures in Ancient Israel." *Biblical Theology Bulletin* 42 (2012).

Maxwell, John C., *The 21 Irrefutable Laws of Leadership: Follow Them and People Will Follow You*, Nashville: Thomas Nelson, 2007.

Metaxas, Eric, *Bonhoeffer*, Nashville, TN: Thomas Nelson, 2010.

Mishnah, Pirkei Avot 1:4, in *The Mishnah: A New Translation*, trans. Jacob Neusner, New Haven: Yale University Press, 1988.

Moody, Dwight L., George Sweeting, *Who Said That?*, Chicago: Moody Press, 1995.

Origen, *On First Principles*, book III, ch. 6, sec. 6, in *Ante-Nicene Fathers*, vol. 4.

Packer, J.I., *Concise Theology: A Guide to Historic Christian Beliefs*, Carol Stream, IL: Tyndale House Publishers, 2001.
    —— *Evangelism and the Sovereignty of God* (Downers Grove, IL: InterVarsity Press, 1961.

Pascal, Blaise, *Memorial*, trans. W. F. Trotter, in *Pensées*, ed.

A.J. Krailsheimer, New York: Penguin Classics, 1966.

Ritzema, Elliot, 300 Quotations for Preachers from the Reformation, Pastorum Series, Bellingham, WA: Lexham Press, 2013.

Rowe, William L., "The Problem of Evil and Some Varieties of Atheism," *American Philosophical Quarterly* 16, no. 4 1979.

"The Role of the Monarchy." The Royal Family. Accessed August 27,2024. https://www.royal.uk/the-role-of-the-monarchy.

Schweitzer, Albert, *An Anthology*, Boston: Beacon Press, 1956.

Seal, David, "Heaven," ed. John D. Barry et al., *The Lexham Bible Dictionary*, Bellingham, WA: Lexham Press, 2016.

Sharma, Robin, *The 5 AM Club: Own Your Morning, Elevate Your Life*, Carlsbad, CA: HarperCollins Leadership, 2018.

Simeon, Charles. *Sermon on Repentance*. Preached at Holy Trinity Church, Cambridge.

Smith, Christian, Melinda Denton, *Soul Searching: The Religious and spiritual Lives of American Teenagers,* New York: Oxford University Press,2006.

Solzhenitsyn, Aleksandr, *The Gulag Archipelago, 1918–1956: An Experiment in Literary Investigation*, trans. Thomas P. Whitney, New York: Harper & Row, 1974.

Sprinkle, Preston, "Is Annihilation an Evangelical Option?" *Preston Sprinkle Blog*, February 3, 2015.

Spurgeon, Charles H., *"Jehovah Tsidkenu: The Lord Our Righteousness,"sermon*no. 395,preached June 2, 1861, at the Metropolitan Tabernacle, Newington; included in *Metropolitan Tabernacle Pulpit*, vol. 7 (London: Passmore & Alabaster, 1861) Strabo, *Geography*, trans. Horace Leonard Jones, Loeb Classical Library, Cambridge, MA: Harvard University Press, 1929.

Strauss, Mark L., *Four Portraits, One Jesus, Grand Rapids, MI: Zondervan, 2007.*

Stott, John R. W., quoted in David L. Edwards and John R. W. Stott, *Evangelical Essentials: A LiberalEvangelical Dialogue*, Leicester, UK: InterVarsity Press, 1988.

Swanson, James, *Dictionary of Biblical Languages with Semantic Domains : Hebrew (Old Testament)*, Oak Harbor: Logos Research Systems, Inc., 1997.

Tozer, A.W., *The Attributes of God*, ed. David F. Edwards, Camp Hill, PA: Christian Publications, 1997

bibliography

Trueman, Carl R., *The Rise and Triumph of the Modern Self*, Wheaton, IL: Crossway, 2020.

——*Strange New World*, Wheaton, IL: Crossway, 2022.

Unger, Merrill Frederick et al., *The New Unger's Bible Dictionary*, Chicago: Moody Press, 1988.

Wright, N.T, *Paul*, London: First Fortress Press, 2009.

——*Paul for Everyone*, London; Ashford Colour Press, 2002.